Southern Living.

The SOUTHERN HERITAGE COOKBOOK LIBRARY

The SOUTHERN HERITAGE
Family
Gatherings
COOKBOOK

OXMOOR HOUSE
Birmingham, Alabama

The Southern Heritage Cookbook Library

Library of Congress Catalog Number: 83-62574
ISBN: 0-8487-0610-2

Manufactured in the United States of America

The Southern Heritage FAMILY GATHERINGS Cookbook

Manager, Editorial Projects: Ann H. Harvey
Southern Living® *Foods Editor*: Jean W. Liles
Production Editor: Joan E. Denman
Foods Editor: Katherine M. Eakin
Director, Test Kitchen: Laura N. Nestelroad
Test Kitchen Home Economists: Pattie B. Booker, Kay E. Clarke,
    Marilyn Hannan, Elizabeth J. Taliaferro
Production Manager: Jerry R. Higdon
Copy Editor: Melinda E. West
Editorial Assistants: Patty E. Howdon, Mary Ann Laurens,
    Karen P. Traccarella
Food Photographer: Jim Bathie
Food Stylist: Sara Jane Ball
Layout Designer: Christian von Rosenvinge
Mechanical Artist: Faith Nance
Research Editors: Evelyn deFrees, Alicia Hathaway

Special Consultants

Art Director: Irwin Glusker
Heritage Consultant: Meryle Evans
Foods Writer: Lillian B. Marshall
Food and Recipe Consultants: Marilyn Wyrick Ingram,
    Audrey P. Stehle

Cover (clockwise from left): Fried Ham with Cream Gravy, Texas Fried
Chicken, Corn Sticks, Birthday Layer Cake, Squash Casserole, and
Perfection Salad. Menu begins on page 74. Photograph by Jim Bathie.

CONTENTS

Introduction 7

Reunions & Homecomings 9

Home for the Holidays 33

Special Days 65

Once in a Lifetime 93

Just Family 119

Acknowledgments 138 Index 140

INTRODUCTION

Over the years, Southerners have devised many occasions for rallying friends and relations to celebrate who they are. This book rejoices with all of them: the enlarged clan reunions so overgrown they must take to public buildings or parks with their annual portable feasts, and the larger-than-life family, gathering under the common flag of unforgotten ethnic derivation. Nor is the old school tie neglected; alumni make yearly pilgrimages to their "homecomings" to keep current with old friends. They arrive from distances short or long, and make convivial, impromptu tailgate meals in the stadium's shadow.

The holiday season from Thanksgiving through New Year's is the primest time for drawing a family together, closely followed by Easter and Passover. We have inherited so many culinary customs that there is scarcely room to add a modern crumb to the traditional menus. We look back in wonder at the celebrations held by hardy souls like the settlers in the Oklahoma Territory and the early Germans in Texas. Hardships notwithstanding, they kept the feasts, adding those touches of Americana native to their new geography.

Special days of family members call for joyful celebration. Birthdays, in particular, are meaningful to Southern families. And unique occurrences, such as silver and golden anniversaries, bring out the most enthusiastic party planning we can muster.

Looking at a given life, we find milestones that we mark with more than the usual fervor. There is the christening, the happy Jewish celebration called Bar Mitzvah, when a boy, at thirteen, becomes a man, and the graduations. The South cries at weddings; tears of joy come down all the way from the engagement announcement through the wedding reception. Married in a garden or her church or in her own home, a Southern bride will have a storehouse of memories; her folks will see to that.

The close family ties that mark the Southern culture is nowhere more in evidence than in the weekly get-together dinner. Whether it be the Jewish Sabbath, for which the cooking is done before sundown the day preceding, or a plain old Sunday dinner where each member knows he'll find his favorite dish, the family gains strength each time it meets. Sometimes we even shut down the kitchen and take Mom out to Sunday dinner!

REUNIONS &
HOMECOMINGS

W hat is it about a Southerner that makes him want to stage mass meetings with his relatives every so often? Or to foregather with a throng with whom he shares sometimes little more than a tribal memory of foreign shores? Or simply to return periodically to his alma mater to talk things over with former classmates on an autumn football afternoon?

Whatever the reasons, they are so deeply ingrained as to be an integral part of Southern life. The Southern culture has undergone social changes similar to those of the rest of the country, yet certain ties with the past are still honored and celebrated. Throughout the region, rural churches have been the focal points of family reunions from the first; the custom spread into the frontier outposts of Texas and Oklahoma from the original coastal settlements.

Earlier this century, by horse and buggy, then by Model T Fords, our great-greats returned to their "home" churches, bearing baskets of food to spread on makeshift tables on the church grounds. They still come, and from greater distances, thanks to superhighways and air travel.

As a natural outgrowth of devotion to church, there arose the "church supper" as fund raiser for needed repairs, Sunday-school rooms, or landscaping, as in our Oklahoma Oyster Supper menu.

The Salzburgers of Ebenezer, Georgia, with 250 years of reunions behind them, may have the longest-running ethnic-related homecoming tradition. But the Norse community of Clifton, Texas, is no less firmly rooted in their 1800s beginnings, no less faithful in remembering the past. The many ethnic heritages that comprise the South are kept in a high state of polish by people who know who they are and where they came from. Southerners are like that. Without shutting others out, they find honor in keeping traditions alive. The South owes much of the richness of its cuisine to their generous sharing.

There is another allegiance with a different slant on the homing instinct: the old school tie. Usually dated for a certain football game in the fall, a college homecoming offers alumni a chance to renew youthful friendships. Renewal is, after all, the reason for all reunions.

MENU OF MENUS

HARDING FAMILY PICNIC

BAIRD FAMILY REUNION

SCANDINAVIAN
SMORGASBORD IN
CLIFTON, TEXAS

A SALZBURGER
HOMECOMING

OKLAHOMA OYSTER
SUPPER

BAYLOR HOMECOMING
OPEN HOUSE

ARKANSAS TAILGATE
PICNIC

*The Imperial Park Drag,
the Harding family carriage,
provides our picnic setting.*

HARDING FAMILY PICNIC

What mixture of tenacity and finesse impelled John Harding and his son, William, to build a gentle empire amid the rolling hills of Middle Tennessee? By 1842, the estate consisted of 3,500 acres; Belle Meade Mansion today surveys only 24 acres and belongs to the state. Their racing stables compiled outstanding records and were known as the oldest and greatest horse nursery in the country. Notable in the collection of horse-drawn carriages in front of the enormous frame carriage house at Belle Meade is the Imperial Park Drag once used for family picnics. Looking something like a stagecoach, it seats four inside and ten on top. The back folded down to form a table, with niches for silverware. This picnic, if necessary, may be otherwise transported.

BELLE MEADE MANSION STUFFED HAM
CORN-ON-THE-COB
COUNTRY GREEN BEANS
HAYDEN SALAD
CORN LIGHT BREAD
FLUFFY YEAST BISCUITS
TURKEY FEET DRESSED EGGS
OSGOOD PIE
DEVIL'S FOOD CAKE

Serves 12 to 14

Reunion of the Harding family of Nashville, Tennessee, c.1890.

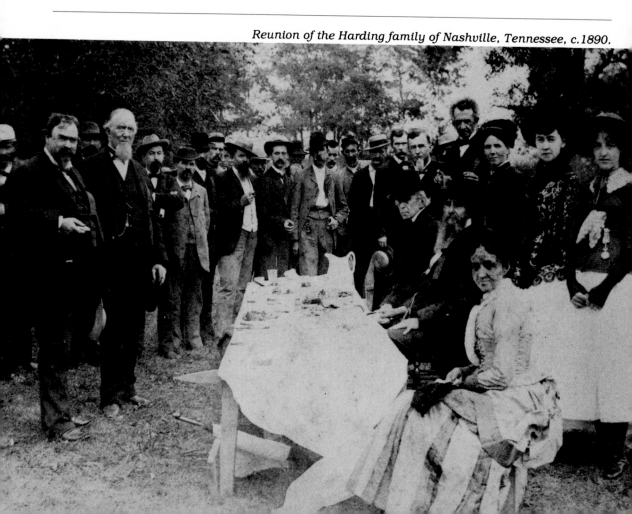

BELLE MEADE MANSION STUFFED HAM

1 (12- to 14-pound) country ham
3 cups finely chopped fresh parsley
3 cups chopped watercress
1 small onion, finely chopped
2 teaspoons dried whole thyme
2 teaspoons dried whole marjoram
1 teaspoon dry mustard
1 teaspoon pepper
½ teaspoon ground mace
6 hard-cooked egg yolks, minced
¼ cup brandy
½ teaspoon ground nutmeg
¾ cup fine dry breadcrumbs

Place ham in a large container; cover with cold water, and soak overnight. Remove ham from water, and drain. Discard water.

Scrub ham thoroughly with a stiff brush, and rinse well with cold water. Place ham in large container; cover with cold water. Bring to a boil; reduce heat, and simmer 4 to 4½ hours, allowing 20 minutes per pound. Turn ham occasionally during cooking time. Set aside to cool. Carefully remove ham from water, and trim all fat. Discard water.

Slit ham lengthwise on side closest to bone, using a sharp boning knife. Place cutting edge of knife toward bone, guiding knife along the length of the bone, continuing around entire bone. Give ham a half turn; insert knife into other end of ham. Repeat procedure. Remove and discard bone from ham.

Combine chopped parsley, watercress, onion, thyme, marjoram, mustard, pepper, and mace. Fill cavity created by bone removal with stuffing mixture. Secure ham around stuffing with wooden picks. Place stuffed ham, cavity-side down, in a shallow roasting pan.

Combine egg yolks, brandy, and nutmeg; mix well. Coat surface of ham with egg mixture; sprinkle with breadcrumbs.

The Harding's Belle Meade mansion, reconstructed in 1853.

Bake, uncovered, at 350° for 1 hour or until breadcrumbs are lightly browned. Cool to room temperature. Refrigerate until thoroughly chilled.

Transfer ham to a serving platter. Cut into thin slices to serve. Yield: 12 to 14 servings.

Note: Leftover ham may be refrigerated for later use.

CORN-ON-THE-COB

14 ears of fresh corn, husks and silks removed
1 tablespoon salt
½ cup butter or margarine, melted
1 tablespoon lemon juice

Place ears of corn in a Dutch oven; cover with cold water. Add salt; bring to a boil. Cover and cook over medium heat 20 minutes or until tender. Drain well.

Combine butter and lemon juice; stir well. Pour butter mixture over corn before serving. Yield: 12 to 14 servings.

COUNTRY GREEN BEANS

4 pounds fresh green beans
1 (12-ounce) package bacon, cut into 2-inch pieces
10 green onions, finely chopped
1 tablespoon water
¾ teaspoon salt
¼ teaspoon pepper
Red pepper relish (optional)

Remove strings from beans; wash and remove tough ends. Set beans aside.

Cook bacon in a large saucepan until crisp; drain on paper towels, and set aside. Reserve ¼ cup bacon drippings in pan.

Sauté onion in reserved bacon drippings until tender. Add beans; cook over medium heat 2 minutes, stirring well. Add water; cover and cook 30 minutes or until beans are tender. Add salt, pepper, and reserved bacon; stir well. Transfer to a serving bowl. Sprinkle relish over top for garnish, if desired. Yield: 12 to 14 servings.

John Harding, founder
of Belle Meade.

Belle Meade's Iroquois won the English Derby in 1881.

HAYDEN SALAD

1 large cabbage, finely
  shredded
4 small onions, chopped
4 cups finely chopped
  tomatoes
2 tablespoons salt
2½ cups sugar
1½ tablespoons celery seeds
1½ teaspoons ground ginger
1½ teaspoons ground
  cinnamon
1½ teaspoons ground mace
1½ teaspoons ground
  turmeric
5 cups vinegar

Combine cabbage, onion, and
tomatoes in a large mixing bowl;
sprinkle with salt, and let stand
30 minutes. Drain well.

Combine remaining ingre-
dients in a large Dutch oven;
bring to a boil. Reduce heat and
simmer 20 minutes. Add
drained vegetables, and simmer
an additional 10 minutes.

Pack mixture into hot sterilized jars, leaving ¼-inch headspace. Cover at once with metal
lids, and screw bands tight. Process in boiling-water bath 5
minutes.

Serve salad as a relish at room
temperature or chilled. Yield:
about 6 pints.

CORN LIGHT BREAD

2 cups yellow cornmeal
1 cup all-purpose flour
1 teaspoon baking powder
1 teaspoon baking soda
½ teaspoon salt
½ cup sugar
3 tablespoons butter or
  margarine, melted
2 cups buttermilk

Combine dry ingredients in a
large mixing bowl; add butter
and buttermilk, mixing well.
Pour batter into a greased 9- x 5-
x 3-inch loafpan. Let mixture
stand 15 minutes. Bake at 350°
for 1 hour. Cut into ½-inch
slices. Serve warm. Yield: one 9-
inch loaf.

FLUFFY YEAST
BISCUITS

1 package dry yeast
½ cup sugar, divided
½ cup warm water (105°
  to 115°)
1 cup cooked, mashed
  potatoes
1 cup milk, scalded
⅔ cup shortening, melted
2 eggs, beaten
1 teaspoon salt
4¼ cups all-purpose flour

Combine yeast, 1 teaspoon
sugar, and water. Let stand 5
minutes or until bubbly.

Combine remaining sugar,
potatoes, milk, shortening,
eggs, and salt; add to yeast mixture, stirring well. Stir in 2 cups
flour. Add enough remaining
flour to make a soft dough.

Turn dough out onto a floured
surface, and knead 10 minutes
or until dough is smooth and
elastic. Place dough in a greased
bowl, turning to grease top.
Cover and let rise in a warm
place (85°), free from drafts, 1
hour or until doubled in bulk.

Punch dough down; shape
into 1½-inch balls. Place balls 1
inch apart on greased baking
sheets. Cover and repeat rising
procedure 1 hour or until doubled in bulk.

Bake at 400° for 12 minutes
or until lightly browned. Yield:
about 5 dozen.

TURKEY FEET DRESSED EGGS

10 hard-cooked eggs
⅓ cup mayonnaise
2 teaspoons prepared
   mustard
¼ teaspoon salt
⅛ teaspoon pepper
Fresh parsley sprigs (optional)

Slice eggs in half lengthwise, and carefully remove yolks. Set egg whites aside.

Mash yolks in a small mixing bowl. Add mayonnaise, mustard, salt, and pepper; mix well. Stuff egg whites with yolk mixture, shaping mixture into a mound using a metal spatula. Using a knife blade, make three indentations in yolk mixture on top of each egg to resemble a turkey foot. Garnish each egg with fresh parsley, if desired. Yield: 12 to 14 servings.

OSGOOD PIE

½ cup butter or margarine
2 cups sugar
4 eggs, separated
1 cup raisins
1 cup chopped pecans
½ teaspoon ground cinnamon
½ teaspoon ground cloves
1 unbaked (9-inch) pastry
   shell

Cream butter; gradually add sugar, beating well. Beat egg yolks until thick and lemon colored; add to butter mixture. Stir in raisins, pecans, cinnamon, and cloves.

Beat egg whites (at room temperature) until stiff peaks form. Gently fold into raisin-pecan mixture. Pour mixture into pastry shell. Bake at 350° for 50 minutes. Cool before slicing. Yield: one 9-inch pie.

In the days of carriage picnics, such delicious temptations as Devil's Food Cake must have traveled in Mother's lap.

DEVIL'S FOOD CAKE

3 cups buttermilk
3 eggs, beaten
1 tablespoon vanilla extract
3¾ cups all-purpose flour
3 cups sugar
1 tablespoon baking soda
¾ teaspoon salt
8 (1-ounce) squares
   unsweetened chocolate
¾ cup butter or margarine
Fluffy White Frosting

Combine buttermilk, eggs, and vanilla in a large mixing bowl; beat at medium speed of an electric mixer until smooth. Set aside.

Combine flour, sugar, soda, and salt; gradually add to buttermilk mixture, beating well after each addition.

Melt chocolate and butter in top of a double boiler. Fold chocolate mixture into batter. Pour batter into 3 greased and floured 9-inch round cakepans.

Bake at 350° for 30 minutes or until a wooden pick inserted in center comes out clean. Cool in pans 10 minutes; remove layers from pans; let cakes cool completely on racks. Spread Fluffy White Frosting between layers and on top and sides of cake. Yield: one 3-layer cake.

Fluffy White Frosting:

1 cup plus 2 tablespoons
   sugar
3 egg whites
½ cup light corn syrup
3 tablespoons water
¼ teaspoon cream of tartar
¼ teaspoon salt
1½ teaspoons vanilla extract

Combine sugar, egg whites (at room temperature), syrup, water, cream of tartar, and salt in top of a large double boiler; beat at low speed of electric mixer 30 seconds or just until blended.

Place over rapidly boiling water; beat constantly at high speed of electric mixer 7 minutes or until stiff peaks form. Remove from heat, and add vanilla; beat 1 minute or until frosting is thick enough to spread. Spread on cooled cake. Yield: frosting for one (9-inch) 3-layer cake.

BAIRD FAMILY REUNION

Since Ridley Baird's descendants started their annual Fourth of July reunion near Mt. Juliet, Tennessee, his tribe has increased so much that the barbecue must be handled professionally. Clarence Bond cooks the pork shoulders, tending the hickory-fired pit, and swabbing the meat with his secret recipe. Custom demands a 5-gallon crock of real lemonade, heavily sugared and served with generous slices of lemon rind for flavor. Baskets of fried chicken, several vegetables, and desserts without number are part of the fare. When a brother brings tomatoes from Alabama, someone will say, "They're good, but Tennessee ones are better."

TENNESSEE SKILLET-FRIED CHICKEN
BARBECUED PORK SHOULDER
SQUASH CASSEROLE
FRIED OKRA
SLICED TOMATOES
CABBAGE SLAW
FRESH PEACH ICE CREAM
TENNESSEE JAM CAKE
PINEAPPLE PIE
LEMONADE

Serves 8 to 10

TENNESSEE SKILLET-FRIED CHICKEN

2 cups all-purpose flour
1 tablespoon salt
1 teaspoon pepper
2 (3½- to 4-pound) broiler-fryers, cut up
2 cups shortening

Combine flour, salt, and pepper in a plastic or paper bag; shake to mix. Place 2 to 3 pieces of chicken in bag; shake well. Repeat procedure with remaining chicken.

Heat shortening in a large heavy skillet to 350°; add chicken, and fry 10 minutes. Reduce heat; cover and continue cooking 5 minutes. Turn chicken pieces, and repeat cooking procedure. Drain on paper towels. Yield: 8 to 10 servings.

The Baird family Fourth of July reunion features sliced tomatoes, Cabbage Slaw, Squash Casserole, Fried Okra, and Lemonade.

BARBECUED PORK SHOULDER

1 medium onion, minced
1 clove garlic, minced
½ cup butter or margarine, melted
1 cup catsup
½ cup vinegar
½ cup water
1 cup firmly packed brown sugar
Zest of 1 lemon, chopped
1½ tablespoons lemon juice
2 tablespoons Worcestershire sauce
1 teaspoon hot sauce
½ teaspoon chili powder
1 (6- to 7-pound) pork shoulder roast

Sauté onion and garlic in butter until tender. Add next 9 ingredients; cook until hot.

Place roast on grill over low coals. Cover grill; open vent. Grill roast 3 hours, turning occasionally.

Baste roast with barbecue sauce. Cook 1 hour or until tender, basting frequently with sauce. Yield: 8 to 10 servings.

Youngster in full regalia celebrates Fourth of July.

Three generations gathered in 1859 to follow tradition on the Fourth of July with flag-flying and fireworks.

SQUASH CASSEROLE

8 large yellow squash, cleaned, boiled, and mashed
1 teaspoon salt
¼ teaspoon pepper
1½ cups buttery round cracker crumbs, divided
2 cups (8 ounces) shredded sharp Cheddar cheese, divided
¼ cup milk
¼ cup butter or margarine

Combine squash, salt, and pepper; stir well. Spoon half of mixture into a lightly greased 2-quart casserole. Sprinkle ¾ cup cracker crumbs and 1½ cups cheese over squash. Repeat layers with remaining squash and cracker crumbs. Pour milk over top, and dot with butter. Bake, uncovered, at 350° for 30 minutes.

Sprinkle remaining ½ cup cheese over top; bake 10 minutes or until cheese melts. Yield: 8 to 10 servings.

FRIED OKRA

3 pounds okra, cleaned
1½ cups yellow cornmeal
1½ teaspoons salt
Vegetable oil

Cut okra crosswise into ½-inch slices; set aside.

Combine cornmeal and salt, mixing well. Dredge sliced okra in cornmeal mixture. Cook in ¼ inch oil over high heat until crisp and lightly browned, stirring occasionally. Drain on paper towels, and serve immediately. Yield: 8 to 10 servings.

CABBAGE SLAW

1 large cabbage, coarsely chopped
1 large green pepper, finely chopped
1 large onion, finely chopped
2 medium carrots, shredded
1 cup sugar
1 cup vinegar
¾ cup vegetable oil
1 teaspoon mustard seeds
1 teaspoon celery seeds
1 teaspoon salt

Combine cabbage, green pepper, onion, carrots, and sugar, mixing well; set aside.

Combine remaining ingredients in a medium saucepan; bring to a boil. Reduce heat, and simmer 5 minutes. Pour over cabbage mixture; toss and chill 3 hours. Drain before serving. Yield: 8 to 10 servings.

FRESH PEACH ICE CREAM

4 cups milk
1 (10-ounce) package large
  marshmallows
2 cups sugar
3 cups mashed fresh peaches
2 cups half-and-half
1 (14-ounce) can sweetened
  condensed milk

Scald milk in a large Dutch oven; add marshmallows, and cook over medium heat until marshmallows melt. Remove from heat. Cool to room temperature. Add remaining ingredients, stirring well.

Pour peach mixture into freezer can of a 1-gallon hand-turned or electric freezer. Freeze according to manufacturer's instructions. Let ice cream ripen at least 1 hour before serving. Yield: about 1 gallon.

TENNESSEE JAM CAKE

1 cup butter or margarine,
  softened
1½ cups sugar
4 eggs
1 teaspoon baking soda
1 cup buttermilk
2 cups all-purpose flour
2 tablespoons cocoa
1 teaspoon ground nutmeg
1 teaspoon ground cinnamon
2 cups blackberry jam
1 teaspoon vanilla extract
1 cup raisins
1 cup chopped pecans
Frosting (recipe follows)

Cream butter in a large mixing bowl; gradually add sugar, beating until light and fluffy. Add eggs, one at a time, beating well after each addition.

Dissolve soda in buttermilk. Combine flour, cocoa, and spices; add to creamed mixture alternately with buttermilk mixture, beginning and ending with flour mixture. Add jam and vanilla, mixing well. Fold in raisins and pecans.

Pour batter into 3 waxed paper-lined, greased and floured 9-inch round cakepans. Bake at 350° for 30 minutes or until a wooden pick inserted in center comes out clean.

Cool in pans 10 minutes. Remove layers from pans to wire racks, and cool completely. Spread frosting between layers and on top and sides of cake. Yield: one 3-layer cake.

Frosting:

3¾ cups sugar, divided
½ cup plus 2 tablespoons
  butter or margarine
1¼ cups milk
Additional milk

Combine 1¼ cups sugar and butter in a 9-inch cast-iron skillet. Cook over medium heat, stirring constantly, until sugar dissolves and butter melts, and mixture becomes golden brown in color. Set aside.

Combine remaining 2½ cups sugar and 1¼ cups milk in a Dutch oven, stirring well. Bring to a boil; stir in reserved sugar mixture. Cook over medium-high heat, stirring occasionally, until mixture reaches 230° (thread stage).

Remove from heat; cool slightly. Beat mixture at medium speed of electric mixer until spreading consistency. Stir in additional milk, if necessary, to maintain spreading consistency. Yield: frosting for one (9-inch) 3-layer cake.

PINEAPPLE PIE

1 cup sugar
3 tablespoons all-purpose
  flour
3 eggs, separated
1 (8-ounce) can crushed
  pineapple, undrained
1 tablespoon butter or
  margarine
1 baked (9-inch) pastry shell
½ teaspoon cream of tartar
¼ cup plus 2 tablespoons
  sugar

Combine 1 cup sugar and flour in a heavy saucepan; add egg yolks, pineapple, and butter, stirring well. Cook mixture over medium heat, stirring constantly, until mixture thickens and comes to a boil. Remove from heat. Cool slightly. Pour filling into pastry shell.

Beat egg whites (at room temperature) and cream of tartar until foamy. Gradually add ¼ cup plus 2 tablespoons sugar, one tablespoon at a time, beating until sugar dissolves and stiff peaks form. Spread meringue over pie, spreading to edges to seal. Bake at 350° for 10 minutes or until meringue is lightly browned. Cool completely. Serve at room temperature. Yield: one 9-inch pie.

LEMONADE

3 quarts water
2 cups sugar
1⅓ cups fresh lemon juice
Lemon slices
Fresh mint leaves (optional)

Combine water and sugar in a large container, stirring until sugar dissolves. Add lemon juice; mix well. Chill thoroughly. Pour into serving glasses, and garnish with lemon slices and mint leaves, if desired. Yield: about 14 cups.

Child enjoys her favorite dessert, 1913 photograph.

17

SCANDINAVIAN SMORGASBORD IN CLIFTON, TEXAS

"**N**orway without the bad winters," the Norse-Americans call Bosque County, Texas. But when Ole Canuteson and seventeen companions came and settled west of Clifton, they also found what they had not had in East Texas: plenty of water and wood for winter fuel. The third Norwegian settlement in Texas, Clifton became the largest. When King Olav V of Norway visited the state in 1982, he could have seen the monument to Cleng Peerson, a Norseman who had made several attempts to plant Norse outposts in other states. The food served at Clifton's Norwegian Smorgasbord is traditional: Now's the time to try authentic Sweet Soup, Norwegian Meat Roll, Lefse, a kind of potato bread, and Krum Kake, a filled pastry cone.

SWEET SOUP
SCANDINAVIAN MEATBALLS
NORWEGIAN MEAT ROLL
SLICES OF SMOKED TURKEY AND HAM
SALMON MOLD
BEET SALAD WITH PICKLED HERRING
BREAD AND BUTTER PICKLES
ASSORTED RELISHES
LEFSE
KRUM KAKE * ROSETTES

Serves 24

SWEET SOUP

1 cup raisins
1 cup golden raisins
20 prunes
25 whole cloves
1 (3-inch) stick cinnamon
3½ quarts water
¼ cup plus 3 tablespoons
  quick-cooking tapioca
1 quart grape juice
½ cup lemon juice
2 cups sugar
2 teaspoons salt

Combine raisins, prunes, cloves, cinnamon, and water in a large Dutch oven; stir well. Bring to a boil. Reduce heat; simmer, uncovered, 30 minutes or until fruit is tender.

Stir in remaining ingredients, and bring to a boil. Reduce heat; cover and simmer 30 minutes, stirring occasionally. Strain soup; discard fruit or save for use in another recipe. Soup may be served hot or cold. Yield: about 6 cups.

SCANDINAVIAN MEATBALLS

3 slices toasted bread, torn
  into small pieces
½ cup milk
2 eggs, beaten
1 tablespoon grated onion
1½ teaspoons salt
½ teaspoon ground nutmeg
½ teaspoon sugar
¼ teaspoon pepper
Dash of garlic salt
1 pound ground round steak
½ pound ground pork
Vegetable oil
1 tablespoon grated onion
1½ tablespoons all-purpose
  flour
2 cups water
2 beef-flavored bouillon
  cubes
¼ teaspoon pepper
¼ cup whipping cream

Combine toasted bread and milk in a large mixing bowl; let stand 1 minute. Add eggs, 1 tablespoon onion, salt, nutmeg, sugar, ¼ teaspoon pepper, garlic salt, and ground meat; mix well. (Mixture may be refrigerated overnight.)

Shape mixture into 1-inch meatballs. Deep fry in hot oil (350°) for 5 minutes or until golden brown. Drain well.

Place 1½ tablespoons hot oil in a large skillet. Sauté remaining 1 tablespoon onion in oil until tender. Add flour, stirring until smooth. Cook 3 minutes or until flour is lightly browned. Gradually add water and bouillon cubes; cook over medium heat, stirring constantly, until thickened and bubbly. Stir in ¼ teaspoon pepper and whipping cream. Add meatballs to sauce. Cover and simmer 20 minutes. Serve immediately. Yield: about 4 dozen.

Smorgasbord: Salmon Mold, Norwegian Meat Roll, sliced meats, and Scandinavian Meatballs.

NORWEGIAN MEAT ROLL

1 (1¼-pound) flank steak
1 tablespoon salt
¾ teaspoon pepper
¾ teaspoon ground ginger
2 tablespoons finely chopped
  onion
⅛ pound ground beef
⅛ pound ground pork
½ pound thinly sliced,
  boneless beef steaks
¼ pound thinly sliced,
  boneless pork steaks

Trim excess fat from flank steak; pound to ⅛-inch thickness using a meat mallet, and set aside.

Combine salt, pepper, and ginger; rub 1 teaspoon mixture into flank steak. Combine remaining salt mixture, onion, and ground meat; mix well.

Place thinly sliced beef evenly over flank steak. Top with pork steaks. Spread ground meat mixture evenly over pork. Roll up jellyroll fashion, and secure with wooden picks. Wrap in cheesecloth, tying ends securely.

Place meat roll in a large Dutch oven. Add water to cover. Bring to a boil. Reduce heat; cover and simmer 1½ to 2 hours. Remove meat roll from water; press between 2 plates. Weight down for 2 hours to press out moisture. Remove and discard cheesecloth and wooden picks. Refrigerate meat roll until well chilled; cut into thin slices, and serve cold. Yield: 24 appetizer servings.

SALMON MOLD

3 envelopes unflavored
  gelatin
¾ cup cold water
6 egg yolks, lightly beaten
1½ teaspoons salt
3 tablespoons prepared
  mustard
¾ teaspoon paprika
¼ cup plus 1 tablespoon
  butter or margarine, melted
2¼ cups milk
½ cup lemon juice
4 (7¾-ounce) cans salmon,
  drained, rinsed, and flaked
Pimiento-stuffed olive slices
  (optional)
Carrot slices (optional)
Fresh parsley sprigs

Soften gelatin in cold water. Combine egg yolks, salt, mustard, and paprika in top of a double boiler. Gradually add butter, milk, and lemon juice; mix well. Cook over boiling water, stirring constantly, 15 minutes. Add gelatin, stirring until dissolved. Gently fold in salmon. Pour mixture into a lightly oiled 5½-cup fish mold. Cover and chill until firm.

Unmold salmon onto a chilled serving plate; decorate fish with olive slices for eyes, and carrot slices for mouth and fins, if desired. Garnish tray with parsley. Serve with melba toast rounds. Yield: 24 appetizer servings.

BEET SALAD WITH PICKLED HERRING

4 (16-ounce) cans whole
  beets, drained and chopped
4 large apples, peeled, cored,
  and coarsely chopped
1 medium onion, peeled and
  coarsely chopped
2 cups vinegar
20 whole allspice
¼ cup sugar
Pickled herring

Combine first 3 ingredients in a large mixing bowl; mix well. Add vinegar, allspice, and sugar; stir well. Cover tightly, and refrigerate overnight. Drain. Serve with pickled herring. Yield: 24 servings.

BREAD AND BUTTER PICKLES

14 large cucumbers, thinly
  sliced
4 large onions, thinly sliced
½ cup pickling salt
5 cups vinegar (5% acidity)
5 cups sugar
2 tablespoons mustard
  seeds
1 tablespoon ground
  turmeric
1½ teaspoons ground cloves

Place cucumbers and onions in a large Dutch oven; sprinkle evenly with salt, and add water to cover. Cover and let stand 3 hours. Drain well.

Combine vinegar, sugar, mustard seeds, turmeric, and cloves in a large container; simmer 5 minutes. Add cucumbers and onions; bring to a boil. Remove from heat.

Pack cucumber mixture into hot sterilized jars, leaving ¼-inch headspace. Cover at once with metal lids, and screw bands tight. Process in a boiling-water bath for 10 minutes. Chill pickles before serving. Yield: 5 quarts.

LEFSE

6 cups cooked, mashed
  potatoes, chilled
3 cups all-purpose flour
¾ cup butter or margarine,
  softened
1 tablespoon sugar
1 tablespoon salt
¾ cup whipping cream
Butter or margarine

Combine potatoes, flour, ¾ cup butter, sugar, and salt; stir well. Gradually add whipping cream, stirring until well blended.

Roll dough to ⅛-inch thickness on a lightly floured surface; cut with a 4-inch biscuit cutter. Fry on a hot greased griddle. Turn cakes when tops are covered with bubbles and edges are lightly browned. Fold cakes in half. Serve hot with butter. Yield: 4 dozen.

KRUM KAKE

4 eggs
⅔ cup superfine sugar
¼ cup plus 2 tablespoons
  all-purpose flour
2 cups whipping cream
2 tablespoons sugar
2 teaspoons vanilla
  extract
Fresh blueberries

Combine eggs and ⅔ cup sugar in a medium mixing bowl; beat well. Gradually add flour, beating until well blended.

Spoon 2 tablespoons batter onto a greased and floured baking sheet. Spread batter with a spatula to form a 4½-inch circle. Repeat procedure with remaining batter, baking two circles at a time. Bake at 400° for 3 minutes or until edges are lightly browned. Remove circles from baking sheet immediately with a long flat spatula. Hold each circle gently, and fold the sides toward the center to form a cone. Stand cone in a tall glass for 2 minutes or until cooled.

Beat whipping cream until foamy. Add 2 tablespoons sugar and vanilla, beating until stiff peaks form. Spoon whipped cream into cones, and top with blueberries. Yield: 2 dozen.

ROSETTES

2 eggs
1 teaspoon sugar
⅛ teaspoon salt
1 cup skim milk
1 cup all-purpose flour
Vegetable oil
Sifted powdered sugar

Beat eggs in a mixing bowl at medium speed of an electric mixer. Gradually add next 3 ingredients; mix well. Add flour; beat until smooth.

Place rosette iron in deep hot oil (375°) about 1 minute. Dip into rosette batter, covering two-thirds of iron. Place in hot oil, and cook 1 minute or until golden brown. Gently shake rosette from iron. Turn and cook 1 minute. Remove with a slotted spoon; drain well. Cool. Repeat procedure with remaining batter. Sprinkle with powdered sugar. Yield: 4 dozen.

Rosette wafer iron, in use over a gas burner in 1905, is still a useful gadget.

A SALZBURGER HOMECOMING

They still call themselves Salzburgers, those German-Americans of Ebenezer, Georgia, out of pride in their ancestors who fled Germany in pursuit of religious freedom in the 1700s. Coming home was in the minds of all who traveled to the Jerusalem Evangelical Lutheran Church in March, 1984, to celebrate the 250th anniversary of the roots put down by those pioneers. Salzburgers participating in the homecoming refreshed their brotherhood by eating hearty meals very much like the family fare enjoyed by those who have gone before.

RED CABBAGE AND APPLES
SAUERBRATEN
HOT GERMAN POTATO SALAD
RAISIN BREAD
GINGERSNAPS
GEORGIA PECAN PIE
SWEET POTATO CUSTARD PIE
ICED TEA

Serves 6 to 8

RED CABBAGE AND APPLES

1 medium-size red cabbage, shredded
2 tablespoons butter or margarine
2 medium-size baking apples, peeled, cored, and thinly sliced
2 tablespoons finely chopped onion
¼ cup dry red wine
3 tablespoons lemon juice
1½ teaspoons salt

Sauté cabbage in butter in a large Dutch oven 10 minutes. Add apples, onion, wine, lemon juice, and salt; stir well. Cover and cook over low heat 1½ hours, stirring occasionally. Serve mixture warm. Yield: 6 to 8 servings.

Between 1767 and 1769, the membership of the Jerusalem Evangelical Lutheran Church built their church using bricks they made themselves.

21

The 250th anniversary of the Georgia Salzburgers.

RAISIN BREAD

2 packages dry yeast
2¼ cups warm water (105°
   to 115°), divided
3 tablespoons sugar
1 tablespoon salt
2 tablespoons shortening
7 cups all-purpose flour,
   divided
2 cups raisins
Butter or margarine, melted

Dissolve yeast in ½ cup warm water in a large mixing bowl, stirring well; let stand 5 minutes or until bubbly. Add remaining warm water, sugar, salt, shortening, and 3½ cups flour; beat well. Stir in raisins and enough remaining flour to make a soft dough.

Turn dough out onto a lightly floured surface; knead 10 minutes or until smooth and elastic. Place dough in a greased bowl, turning to grease top. Cover and let rise in a warm place (85°), free from drafts, 2 hours or until doubled in bulk.

Punch dough down; turn out onto a lightly floured surface. Divide dough in half, and shape each into a loaf. Place in 2 greased 9- x 5- x 3-inch loafpans. Cover and repeat rising procedure 45 minutes or until doubled in bulk.

Bake at 350° for 40 minutes or until loaves sound hollow when tapped. Remove from pans immediately; cool on wire racks. Brush tops with melted butter. Yield: 2 loaves.

SAUERBRATEN

1 clove garlic, minced
1 teaspoon salt
¼ teaspoon pepper
1 (3½- to 4-pound) beef
   shoulder roast
1 cup water
1 cup vinegar
1 medium onion, thinly
   sliced
¼ cup sugar
1 teaspoon whole
   peppercorns
2 bay leaves
¼ cup all-purpose flour
2 tablespoons vegetable oil

Combine garlic, salt, and pepper; rub entire surface of roast with mixture. Place in a large container.

Combine water, vinegar, onion, sugar, peppercorns, and bay leaves in a large saucepan. Cook over medium heat 5 minutes. Pour sauce over meat; cover and refrigerate at least 7 days, turning meat once a day.

Remove roast, reserving marinade. Remove and discard peppercorns and bay leaves from marinade. Dredge roast in flour. Brown roast on all sides in hot oil in a large Dutch oven. Add reserved marinade; bring to a boil. Reduce heat; cover and simmer 3 hours or until roast is tender. Remove roast to a serving platter. Yield: 6 to 8 servings.

HOT GERMAN POTATO SALAD

2 pounds medium-size
   red potatoes
6 hard-cooked eggs, finely
   chopped
1¼ cups mayonnaise
½ cup chopped onion
1 tablespoon celery
   seeds
½ teaspoon salt
4 slices bacon
¼ cup cider vinegar
¼ cup hot water
¼ cup sugar

Scrub potatoes. Cook in boiling water 25 minutes or until tender. Drain and cool slightly. Peel potatoes, and cut into ¾-inch cubes. Set aside to cool completely.

Combine chopped eggs, mayonnaise, onion, celery seeds, salt, and cooled potatoes in a large mixing bowl; toss gently to mix. Set aside.

Cook bacon in a large skillet until crisp; remove bacon, reserving drippings in skillet. Crumble bacon, and set aside. Add vinegar, water, and sugar to pan drippings, stirring well. Cook mixture over medium heat until sugar dissolves. Add potato mixture, mixing well. Cook until thoroughly heated. Sprinkle with reserved bacon. Serve hot. Yield: 6 to 8 servings.

22

GINGERSNAPS

¾ cup shortening
1 cup sugar
1 egg
¼ cup molasses
2 cups all-purpose flour
1 teaspoon baking soda
1 teaspoon ground
   cinnamon
1 teaspoon ground ginger
1 teaspoon ground cloves
Additional sugar

Cream shortening; gradually add 1 cup sugar, beating until light and fluffy. Add egg and molasses; beat well.

Sift together flour, soda, and spices. Add to creamed mixture, mixing well.

Shape dough into ¾-inch balls. Roll balls in sugar. Place on greased baking sheets; lightly flatten balls. Bake at 375° for 8 minutes or until browned. (Tops will crack.) Place on wire racks to cool. Store in an airtight container. Yield: 6 dozen.

Salzburger reunion is incomplete without Raisin Bread and Gingersnaps.

GEORGIA PECAN PIE

½ cup butter or margarine,
   softened
1 cup sugar
1 cup firmly packed
   brown sugar
2 tablespoons all-purpose
   flour
3 eggs, beaten
¾ cup milk
1½ cups chopped pecans
1 teaspoon vanilla extract
1 unbaked (9-inch)
   pastry shell

Cream butter; gradually add sugar, beating well. Add flour, eggs, and milk; beat well. Stir in pecans and vanilla. Pour mixture into pastry shell. Bake at 350° for 1 hour. Cool before slicing. Yield: one 9-inch pie.

SWEET POTATO CUSTARD PIE

¼ cup butter or margarine,
   softened
1 cup sugar
¼ teaspoon salt
3 eggs, separated
3 tablespoons lemon juice
1 tablespoon grated
   orange rind
½ teaspoon ground
   nutmeg
3 large sweet potatoes,
   cooked and mashed
1 cup half-and-half
1 unbaked (9-inch) pastry
   shell
¼ cup butter or margarine,
   melted
¼ cup firmly packed dark
   brown sugar
¾ cup chopped pecans

Combine ¼ cup butter, 1 cup sugar, salt, and egg yolks in a large mixing bowl; beat well. Add lemon juice, orange rind, nutmeg, potatoes, and half-and-half; beat until well blended. Beat egg whites (at room temperature) until stiff peaks form. Fold into sweet potato mixture. Pour filling into pastry shell.

Combine ¼ cup melted butter, brown sugar, and pecans; mix well. Sprinkle pecan mixture evenly over top of filling. Bake at 425° for 10 minutes. Reduce heat to 350°; bake an additional 30 minutes or until a knife inserted in center comes out clean. Cool before serving. Yield: one 9-inch pie.

OKLAHOMA OYSTER SUPPER

Settlers found the Oklahoma Country rich in rivers and streams, greatly increasing the desirability of the land. Second- and third-generation Oklahomans were able to enjoy not only the native fresh water fish as their elders had done, but also "imported" oysters from the coast. Bean suppers, box suppers, chili suppers . . . all have been used to raise money for churches and charities. On this American custom was built the Oklahoma Oyster Supper, with oysters prepared in several ways. An early oyster supper at First Baptist Church in Oklahoma City netted $200. By 1899, the Chesapeake Fish and Oyster Depot there was thriving.

ANGELS ON HORSEBACK
DEVILED OYSTERS
FRIED OYSTERS
FRIED TROUT
TARTAR SAUCE
SEAFOOD SAUCE
HUSH PUPPIES
LEMON SQUARES

Serves 12

ANGELS ON HORSEBACK

14 to 16 slices bacon, halved
   crosswise
2 (12-ounce) containers fresh
   Select oysters, drained
2 cups yellow cornmeal
1 teaspoon salt
½ teaspoon pepper
½ cup milk
2 eggs
Vegetable oil

Wrap a bacon half around each oyster; secure with a wooden pick through oyster.

Combine cornmeal, salt, and pepper; dredge oysters in meal mixture. Combine milk and eggs; beat well. Dip oysters into milk mixture; dredge again in meal mixture. Deep fry in hot oil (375°) until golden brown; drain on paper towels. Serve warm with Seafood Sauce. Yield: 12 appetizer servings.

Supper is Deviled Oysters in shells, Angels on Horseback, and Fried Oysters. Tartar or Seafood Sauce adds zest.

DEVILED OYSTERS

1 medium-size green pepper, chopped
¾ cup chopped onion
¾ cup sweet pickle relish, drained
½ cup chopped sweet red pepper
½ cup chopped fresh parsley
¾ cup butter or margarine, divided
2 cups soft breadcrumbs, divided
1 tablespoon Worcestershire sauce
½ teaspoon salt
⅛ teaspoon pepper
1 egg, beaten
3 (12-ounce) containers fresh Select oysters, drained
Paprika

Sauté green pepper, onion, pickle relish, red pepper, and parsley in ½ cup butter in a large skillet until tender. Stir in 1 cup breadcrumbs, Worcestershire sauce, salt, pepper, egg, and oysters. Spoon evenly into 12 seashells or ramekins. Cover; chill at least 1 hour.

Sauté 1 cup breadcrumbs in remaining butter until lightly browned. Top oyster mixture with sautéed breadcrumbs; sprinkle with paprika. Place shells on baking sheets. Bake at 350° for 30 to 35 minutes. Serve hot. Yield: 12 servings.

FRIED OYSTERS

2 (12-ounce) containers fresh Select oysters, drained
2 cups cracker crumbs
3 eggs
1 teaspoon salt
½ teaspoon pepper
Vegetable oil

Dredge oysters in cracker crumbs. Combine eggs, salt, and pepper; beat well. Dip oysters in egg; dredge in cracker crumbs. Repeat dipping and dredging procedure.

Deep fry oysters in hot oil (375°) until golden brown; drain on paper towels. Serve hot with Seafood Sauce. Yield: 12 appetizer servings.

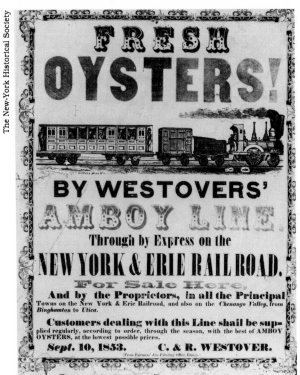

The New York and Erie delivered oysters, 1853.

FRIED TROUT

2 to 2½ pounds trout fillets
1 cup all-purpose flour
7 egg yolks, well beaten
2 cups fine, dry breadcrumbs
Vegetable oil

Dredge both sides of fish in flour. Dip fish into egg yolk, coating entire surface. Dredge fish again in breadcrumbs.

Carefully drop fish into deep hot oil (370°). Fry until fish float to the top and are golden brown. Drain well on paper towels. Serve hot with Tartar Sauce. Yield: 12 servings.

TARTAR SAUCE

2 cups mayonnaise
¼ cup minced or grated dill pickle
¼ cup minced or grated onion
2 teaspoons prepared horseradish

Combine all ingredients in a small mixing bowl, mixing well. Cover; chill several hours before serving. Yield: about 2½ cups.

Richard and Eliza Reynolds lived on Creek Indian land southeast of Muskogee before statehood came to Oklahoma. Eliza's recipe for fried fish advised against frying in butter alone, as it "takes out the sweetness and gives a bad color." She suggested lard or beef drippings or equal parts lard and butter; however, she preferred salt pork drippings. Any fish might be dredged in Indian meal except trout and perch.

A picnic of the Haworth Church of Christ, McCurtin County, Oklahoma, 1913.

SEAFOOD SAUCE

1 cup chili sauce
1 cup catsup
¼ cup plus 2 tablespoons
  lemon juice
2 tablespoons mayonnaise
2 teaspoons Worcestershire
  sauce
1 teaspoon grated onion
½ teaspoon salt
6 drops hot sauce
Dash of pepper

Combine all ingredients, stirring until smooth. Cover and chill at least 2 hours. Serve sauce with seafood. Yield: about 3 cups.

HUSH PUPPIES

3½ cups water
2 cups cornmeal
1 teaspoon baking powder
1 tablespoon sugar
1 teaspoon salt
1 medium onion, finely
  chopped
¼ cup butter or margarine,
  softened
Vegetable oil

Bring water to a boil in a small Dutch oven. Combine cornmeal, baking powder, sugar, salt, and onion; slowly add to boiling water, stirring constantly until mixture is smooth. Remove from heat; add butter, stirring until melted. Cool mixture 10 minutes.

Shape batter into 2- x 1-inch oblong rolls. Deep fry in hot oil (375°), cooking only a few at a time. Fry until hush puppies are golden brown. Drain well on paper towels. Serve hot. Yield: about 3½ dozen.

LEMON SQUARES

2 cups all-purpose flour
½ cup sifted powdered
  sugar
1 cup butter or margarine
4 eggs
2 cups sugar
1 tablespoon sifted
  powdered sugar
¼ cup lemon juice

Combine flour and ½ cup powdered sugar in a large mixing bowl; stir well. Cut in butter with a pastry blender until mixture resembles coarse meal. Spoon into a 13- x 9- x 2-inch baking dish; press firmly into bottom of dish. Bake at 350° for 20 minutes. Remove from oven.

Combine eggs, sugar, 1 tablespoon powdered sugar, and lemon juice; beat well. Pour egg mixture over hot crust. Continue baking at 350° for 25 minutes or until lightly browned. Let cool, and cut into 1½-inch squares. Yield: about 4 dozen.

BAYLOR HOMECOMING OPEN HOUSE

When Baylor University in Waco, Texas, celebrated its 73rd homecoming in 1982, it was believed to have been one of the largest in the country. Retired history professor Dr. Ralph Lynn, class of '32, and his wife, Bessie Mae, were in their element. They attended their class dinner, of course, but mainly it was time for the open house they give each year for one to two hundred (they never know how many) people. Mrs. Lynn now has some of the food catered, but all else remains the same. Her spiced tea is famous; she has copies printed for the inevitable requests.

CHICKEN SANDWICHES
OLIVE-MUSTARD SANDWICHES
CUCUMBER-CREAM CHEESE SANDWICHES
PECAN TARTS
APRICOT CREAM TARTS
SPICED HOT TEA

Serves 16 to 20

CHICKEN SANDWICHES

1 cup chopped cooked chicken
¼ cup finely chopped green pepper
¼ cup chopped blanched almonds
2 tablespoons whipping cream
¼ teaspoon prepared mustard
¼ teaspoon salt
⅛ teaspoon pepper
16 slices white bread
Green pepper stars

Combine chicken, green pepper, and almonds in a medium mixing bowl; mix well. Combine whipping cream, mustard, salt, and pepper; add to chicken mixture, mixing well. Chill.

Remove crust from bread. Spread chicken mixture evenly over 8 slices of bread. Place remaining bread slices over chicken mixture to make sandwiches. Cut each sandwich into 4 squares. Garnish cut sandwiches with green pepper stars. Yield: 32 appetizer sandwiches.

The dainty sandwiches gracing this tea table are Olive-Mustard (front), Chicken (center), and Cucumber-Cream Cheese.

OLIVE-MUSTARD SANDWICHES

1 cup butter, softened
1 cup chopped
    pimiento-stuffed olives
3 hard-cooked eggs,
    chopped
1 tablespoon dry mustard
⅛ teaspoon salt
⅛ teaspoon paprika
18 slices whole wheat bread
12 slices white bread
Pimiento-stuffed olive slices

Cream butter; add chopped olives, eggs, mustard, salt, and paprika, stirring until smooth.
Trim crust from bread. Spread olive mixture on two slices of whole wheat bread and two slices of white bread. Stack slices alternately beginning with wheat bread. Top with a slice of wheat bread. Cut sandwich in half lengthwise and in 5 slices crosswise. Repeat procedure with remaining bread slices and olive-mustard mixture. Garnish sandwiches with olive slices. Yield: 5 dozen appetizer sandwiches.

Floats are a fun part of a college homecoming parade. This 1961 float was built by Alpha Kappa Psi, a men's social club at Baylor University.

CUCUMBER-CREAM CHEESE SANDWICHES

1 small onion, peeled
1 medium cucumber, peeled
2 stalks celery
2 (8-ounce) packages cream
    cheese, softened
¼ teaspoon salt
10 drops hot sauce
1 (16-ounce) loaf thin-sliced
    white bread
Mayonnaise
Cucumber slices (optional)

Grate onion, cucumber, and celery. Drain well. Combine vegetables, cream cheese, salt, and hot sauce in a medium mixing bowl; beat until smooth.
Remove crust from bread, and cut each slice into four triangles. Coat each piece lightly with mayonnaise. Spread filling on bread slices. Garnish with cucumber slices, if desired. Yield: about 3½ dozen open-faced appetizer sandwiches.
Alternate method: Position knife blade in food processor bowl; add onion, cucumber, and celery. Process 3 to 5 seconds. Stop processor, and scrape sides of bowl with a rubber spatula. Process an additional 3 to 5 seconds or until vegetables are finely chopped. Remove vegetables, and drain well.

PECAN TARTS

3 eggs, beaten
1 cup light corn syrup
1 tablespoon butter or
    margarine, melted
½ teaspoon vanilla extract
1 cup sugar
1 tablespoon all-purpose flour
Pastry (recipe follows)
¼ cup plus 2 tablespoons
    butter or margarine,
    softened
½ cup finely chopped pecans

Combine eggs, syrup, melted butter, and vanilla in a large mixing bowl. Combine sugar and flour; add to egg mixture, mixing well. Set aside.
Roll pastry into a rectangle ¼-inch thick on a lightly floured surface. Spread pastry with softened butter, leaving a 1-inch margin at edges. Fold in thirds like a letter; pinch edges to seal. Turn sealed edges to bottom.
Roll again to ⅛-inch thickness on a lightly floured surface. (If butter breaks through dough, flour lightly and continue rolling.) Cut into 4-inch rounds; fit rounds into 2¾-inch muffin tins. Press flat to cover sides of tins; trim pastry along edge of tin with a sharp knife. Prick bottom of each shell.
Sprinkle each unbaked tart shell with 1 teaspoon pecans. Spoon 2 tablespoons reserved filling into each tart shell. Bake at 350° for 35 minutes. Cool completely before removing from pans. Yield: 2 dozen.

Pastry:

3 cups all-purpose flour
1½ teaspoons salt
1 cup shortening
6 to 8 tablespoons ice water

Combine flour and salt in a large mixing bowl; cut in shortening with a pastry blender until mixture resembles coarse meal. Cover and chill 1 hour.
Sprinkle ice water evenly over surface, 1 tablespoon at a time; stir with a fork until dry ingredients are moistened. Shape dough into a ball. Chill before using. Yield: pastry for 2 dozen (2¾-inch) tart shells.

Texas Collection, Baylor University

Marching band, pretty girls, and flowery float from Baylor Homecoming Parade, 1946.

APRICOT CREAM TARTS

1 (17-ounce) can apricot
   halves, undrained
2 tablespoons lemon juice
1 envelope unflavored gelatin
¼ cup water
½ cup sugar
¼ teaspoon salt
¾ cup whipping cream
24 baked (2¾-inch)
   commercial tart shells
Additional whipped cream
Toasted coconut

Drain apricots, reserving ½ cup syrup. Set syrup aside.

Press apricots through a food mill or sieve. Combine apricot puree and lemon juice; stir well, and set aside.

Sprinkle gelatin over water. Let stand 5 minutes; stir gently. Combine apricot syrup, apricot puree mixture, gelatin, sugar, and salt in a medium mixing bowl; stir well. Chill until partially set.

Pour ¾ cup whipping cream into a chilled bowl, and beat until stiff peaks form. Fold into apricot mixture. Spoon 2 tablespoons mixture into each tart shell. Chill thoroughly. Dollop with whipped cream, and sprinkle with toasted coconut before serving. Yield: 2 dozen.

SPICED HOT TEA

1 (3-inch) stick cinnamon,
   crushed
2 teaspoons whole cloves
6 quarts water
6 tea bags
3 cups sugar
1 (12-ounce) can frozen
   orange juice, thawed and
   undiluted
1 (6-ounce) can frozen
   lemonade, thawed and
   undiluted

Wrap cinnamon and cloves securely in cheesecloth; place in a stockpot, and add water. Bring to a boil; remove from heat, and add tea bags. Cover and let stand 10 minutes. Remove and discard tea bags and spices.

Add sugar, orange juice, and lemonade, stirring until sugar dissolves. Let stand 2 hours. Heat tea before serving. Yield: about 6 quarts.

ARKANSAS TAILGATE PICNIC

Win, lose, or draw, with the publication of this menu, the University of Arkansas Razorbacks may be the only team in the Southwest Conference to boast a sandwich named in its honor. Roast pork on bread of brown rice (another Arkansas product), the Razorback sandwich is destined for fame. Next time the Baylor Bears of Waco, or any other team without its own sandwich, meets the Arkansas eleven, they'll have to reckon with rabid fans who have driven for miles and celebrated with a tailgate lunch like this: sandwiches, salad, cookies, iced tea—or beer.

RAZORBACK ROAST SANDWICHES
BROWN RICE BREAD
PIQUANT GREEN BEAN SALAD
ARKANSAS TRAVELERS
FROSTED SPICE BARS
BEER * ICED TEA

Serves 8

RAZORBACK ROAST SANDWICHES

½ cup soy sauce
½ cup sherry
2 cloves garlic, minced
1 tablespoon dry mustard
1 teaspoon ground ginger
1 teaspoon dried whole thyme
1 (4- to 5-pound) rolled pork roast
16 slices Brown Rice Bread
Mayonnaise, mustard, and/or catsup
Tomato slices
Lettuce leaves

Combine first 6 ingredients; stir well. Place mixture and roast in a large plastic bag with seal; close bag. Marinate overnight in refrigerator, turning bag occasionally.

Remove meat from marinade, reserving marinade. Place roast on rack in a shallow roasting pan. Insert meat thermometer into meaty part of roast. Bake, uncovered, at 350° for 2½ hours or until thermometer reaches 170°, basting frequently with marinade. Let stand 10 minutes. Slice for sandwiches.

Spread 8 slices of Brown Rice Bread with desired condiments. Top with pork, tomato, and lettuce. Cover with remaining 8 slices. Yield: 8 sandwiches.

Arkansas Tailgate Picnic menu with vintage Ford wagon.

The Arkansas Razorbacks scrimmage before a small crowd, c.1935.

BROWN RICE BREAD

2 packages dry yeast
1 teaspoon sugar
½ cup warm water (105° to 115°)
3½ cups all-purpose flour
3½ cups whole wheat flour
¾ cup instant nonfat dry milk powder
⅓ cup sugar
1 tablespoon salt
½ cup shortening
1½ cups warm water (105° to 115°)
3 cups cooked warm brown rice
Additional all-purpose flour

Dissolve yeast and 1 teaspoon sugar in ½ cup warm water; stir well, and let stand 5 minutes.

Combine flour, milk powder, ⅓ cup sugar, and salt in a large mixing bowl; stir well. Cut in shortening with a pastry blender until mixture resembles coarse meal. Stir in yeast mixture, 1½ cups warm water, and warm rice to make a soft dough.

Turn dough out onto a lightly floured surface. Knead 10 minutes or until smooth and elastic, working in additional flour as needed. Place dough in a greased bowl, turning to grease top. Cover and let rise in a warm place (85°), free from drafts, 1 hour or until doubled in bulk.

Punch dough down, and turn out onto a lightly floured surface; divide into 3 equal portions, shaping each into a loaf. Place each loaf in a greased 8½- x 4½ x 3-inch loafpan. Cover; repeat rising procedure 1 hour or until doubled in bulk.

Bake at 350° for 35 minutes or until loaves sound hollow when tapped. Remove bread from pans, and cool on wire racks. Cut into thin slices for sandwiches. Yield: 3 loaves.

Here the Fort Smith, Arkansas, football team of 1906 poses for a picture that will be a hit at the next class reunion.

FROSTED SPICE BARS

½ cup golden raisins
2 eggs
1 cup firmly packed brown sugar
1 cup all-purpose flour
½ teaspoon salt
½ teaspoon baking powder
½ teaspoon ground cinnamon
⅛ teaspoon ground cloves
¼ cup butter or margarine, melted
½ cup chopped pecans
Frosting (recipe follows)
¼ cup chopped pecans

Soak raisins in hot water to cover 15 minutes or until raisins are plumped. Drain well, and set aside.

Beat eggs in a large mixing bowl until light and foamy. Add sugar, beating well.

Sift together flour, salt, baking powder, cinnamon, and cloves. Add to egg mixture, stirring well. Stir in butter, ½ cup pecans, and raisins. Pour into a greased and floured 8-inch square baking pan.

Bake at 350° for 25 to 30 minutes. Cool completely. Spread top with frosting; sprinkle with ¼ cup chopped pecans. Cut into 2-inch squares. Yield: 16 squares.

Frosting:

2 tablespoons butter or margarine
1½ cups sifted powdered sugar
1 tablespoon hot water
1 teaspoon half-and-half
½ teaspoon vanilla extract

Brown butter lightly in a heavy saucepan. Remove from heat. Add sugar, hot water, half-and-half, and vanilla, stirring until smooth. Yield: frosting for one (8-inch) square cake.

PIQUANT GREEN BEAN SALAD

3 (16-ounce) cans French-style green beans, drained
½ cup mayonnaise
2 tablespoons prepared mustard
1 tablespoon prepared horseradish
1 tablespoon finely chopped onion
1 tablespoon vinegar
½ teaspoon salt
Pimiento strips (optional)

Combine beans, mayonnaise, mustard, horseradish, onion, vinegar, and salt in a large mixing bowl; stir until well blended. Cover and refrigerate 4 hours. Garnish with pimiento strips, if desired. Yield: 8 servings.

ARKANSAS TRAVELERS

½ cup butter or margarine, softened
½ cup sugar
½ cup firmly packed brown sugar
1 egg
½ teaspoon vanilla extract
½ cup creamy peanut butter
1½ cups all-purpose flour
1 teaspoon baking powder
½ cup finely chopped pecans

Cream butter; gradually add sugar, beating well. Add egg and vanilla, mixing well. Stir in peanut butter.

Combine flour and baking powder; add to peanut butter mixture, beating well. Stir in pecans. Shape into 1-inch balls; place 2 inches apart on ungreased baking sheets. Dip a fork in water, and flatten balls to ½-inch thickness.

Bake at 350° for 10 minutes or until lightly browned. Remove to wire racks, and cool. Yield: about 3½ dozen.

HOME FOR THE HOLIDAYS

T here is no doubt about it: the homing instinct peaks at holiday time. The college freshman, away for the longest time in her young life, the careerist working several states away, the aunt alone who needs including—they come home. Thanksgiving, the Christmas and New Year's holidays, and Easter are for drawing in, the family gaining strength by sharing the happenings and ideas that are constantly shaping their lives. What does not change is the warm and caring atmosphere of the Southern home place.

Heading home for the holidays may entail weeks or months of planning; vacation time is hoarded, along with the wherewithal to finance the trip. In colonial days going home was as simple as hitching horse to carriage for a few miles overland.

The South's history of combining religious and secular observances of Christmas and Easter was not shared by the North. The Puritan fathers believed it improper to hail the holy days with merrymaking, although New Year's and Thanksgiving were kept as enthusiastically as in the South, with feasting and games, fireworks and spiritous toasts.

The Southern ingathering for the holidays takes cues from the rich palette of ethnic and geographic colorations that comprise the region. The English tradition of much of the population is straight off the Eastern Seaboard, right down to the plum pudding as a finale to a Thanksgiving menu. Different ethnic and geographic roots dictate the foods served by the descendants of those pioneers who spread out and settled the South and West to embrace or to co-exist with the Mexican and Indian cultures.

This chapter is nostalgia unabashed. Why not relive the glorious feasts from the grand plantations like Belle Meade, Hope Farm, and Middleton Place? Why not think hard about the Germans in Texas and the settlers of the Oklahoma Territories who wrested their holiday observances out of hard and bewildering times, happy to have their families drawn in a tight circle? Those families were as real as ours are today; we are like them in many ways, consciously or not. And one of the important resemblances is in the holiday foods we Southern families eat.

MENU OF MENUS

SOUTHERN MARYLAND
EASTER DINNER

TRADITIONAL
THANKSGIVING DINNER

THANKSGIVING TEA
PARTY

GERMAN-STYLE
CHRISTMAS EVE SUPPER

OKLAHOMA TERRITORY
CHRISTMAS DINNER

CHRISTMAS EGGNOG AT
HOPE FARM

MIDDLETON PLACE
CHRISTMAS DINNER

PROSPERO AÑO NUEVO

GREEK NEW YEAR'S
DINNER

SOUTHERN MARYLAND EASTER DINNER

Although its fame is spreading, Maryland Stuffed Ham is still most used and enjoyed by those close to its origin, the two Catholic counties of Charles and St. Mary's in southern Maryland. Jesuit priests established St. Thomas Manor there in 1658 on what was once an estate of 4,000 acres. It is also the site of St. Ignatius Church, an early center of Catholic church and mission life. The story of stuffed ham goes like this: The good priests, having tired of a winter diet of plain cured ham and seeing such spring greens as cress, onions, and kale heralding spring in the lowlands, combined ham and greens into one glorious dish. That dish is the starting point for this menu which is traditionally served at Easter in southern Maryland.

SOUTHERN MARYLAND
STUFFED HAM
CREAMED RED POTATOES
BAKED TOMATO HALVES
FRILLY DEVILED EGGS
BISCUITS SUPREME
CARDINAL PUDDING

Serves 8

SOUTHERN MARYLAND STUFFED HAM

1 (12- to 15-pound) country ham
3 pounds fresh spinach, chopped
1 pound turnip or mustard greens, chopped
1 bunch celery, chopped
1 bunch green onions, chopped
3 tablespoons chopped fresh chives
3 tablespoons celery seeds
2 tablespoons pepper
2 to 4 teaspoons hot sauce
Cheesecloth

Place ham in a very large stock pot; cover with cold water. Bring to a boil. Reduce heat, and simmer 20 minutes. Drain; cool ham slightly. Remove skin and fat from ham, and discard.

Combine spinach, greens, celery, onion, and chives. Cover with boiling water; let stand 5 to 10 minutes. Drain well, and rinse in cold water. Drain well.

Add celery seeds, pepper, and hot sauce to spinach mixture, mixing well. Set aside.

Starting at butt end of ham, make a row of lengthwise slits, 2 inches long, completely through ham. Repeat rows over entire top of ham, making sure slits do not cut into other slits. Pack spinach mixture into slits. Place excess spinach mixture on top of ham.

Wrap stuffed ham in cheesecloth; tie ends with string. Place ham in a large stock pot; cover with water. Bring water to a boil. Reduce heat, and simmer 2½ to 3 hours.

Remove stock pot from heat; set aside. Allow ham to cool 2 hours in cooking liquid. Remove ham, and discard liquid. Allow ham to cool to room temperature. Chill overnight. Remove cheesecloth.

Transfer ham to a serving platter. Cut diagonally across the grain into thin slices to serve. Yield: 8 servings.
Note: Leftover ham may be refrigerated for later use.

CREAMED RED POTATOES

8 medium-size red potatoes, peeled and cubed
2 cups half-and-half
½ teaspoon salt
¼ teaspoon pepper
¼ cup butter or margarine, softened
2 teaspoons chopped fresh chives
2 teaspoons chopped fresh parsley

Combine first 4 ingredients in a Dutch oven. Cook over low heat 35 minutes or until potatoes are fork tender (do not allow mixture to boil). Stir in butter; sprinkle with chives and parsley. Serve immediately. Yield: 8 servings.

Southern Maryland Stuffed Ham on plate with Baked Tomato Halves and Creamed Red Potatoes. Add Frilly Deviled Eggs and Biscuits Supreme.

BAKED TOMATO HALVES

4 medium tomatoes, cut in half crosswise
1 tablespoon sugar
1 teaspoon salt
⅛ teaspoon pepper
¾ cup soft breadcrumbs
3 tablespoons butter or margarine, melted
2 tablespoons chopped fresh parsley

Place tomato halves, cut side up, in a 12- x 8- x 2-inch baking dish. Combine sugar, salt, and pepper; sprinkle evenly over cut surface of each tomato half.

Combine breadcrumbs, butter, and parsley, tossing well. Sprinkle breadcrumb mixture evenly over cut surface of each tomato. Pour ½ inch water around tomatoes in dish. Bake at 350° for 20 minutes or until breadcrumbs are lightly browned. Transfer to a warm serving platter. Serve warm. Yield: 8 servings.

FRILLY DEVILED EGGS

6 hard-cooked eggs
2½ tablespoons mayonnaise
3 tablespoons finely chopped sweet pickle
⅛ teaspoon salt
Dash of pepper
1 (3-ounce) package cream cheese, softened
½ to 1 teaspoon milk
Food coloring
Shredded lettuce

Slice eggs in half lengthwise, and carefully remove yolks; set aside egg whites.

Combine yolks and mayonnaise in a small mixing bowl; mash well. Add pickle, salt, and pepper, mixing well. Stuff egg whites with yolk mixture. Place stuffed eggs, yolk side down, on waxed paper. Set aside.

Beat cream cheese; add milk, and beat until mixture reaches spreading consistency. Tint cream cheese to desired color. Decorate eggs with cream cheese mixture using a pastry bag. Transfer eggs to a serving tray lined with shredded lettuce. Chill. Yield: 8 servings.

BISCUITS SUPREME

2 cups all-purpose flour
1 tablespoon plus 1 teaspoon baking powder
2 teaspoons sugar
½ teaspoon salt
½ teaspoon cream of tartar
½ cup shortening
⅔ cup milk

Combine first five ingredients in a medium mixing bowl; stir well. Cut in shortening with a pastry blender until mixture resembles coarse meal. Gradually add milk, stirring until dry ingredients are moistened.

Turn dough out onto a floured surface; knead 4 to 5 times. Roll dough to ½-inch thickness; cut with a 2-inch biscuit cutter. Bake on a greased baking sheet at 450° for 10 minutes or until lightly browned. Yield: about 1½ dozen.

St. Ignatius Church at Chapel Point, Maryland, built in 1798 by Rev. Charles Sewall.

CARDINAL PUDDING

1 (10-ounce) commercial
   angel food cake
About ¼ cup red currant jelly
¼ cup whole blanched
   almonds
¼ cup chopped citron
1 cup red wine
¾ cup sugar, divided
4 cups milk, divided
3 eggs, beaten
2½ tablespoons all-purpose
   flour
⅛ teaspoon baking soda
1 teaspoon vanilla extract

Split cake in half crosswise. Spread cut side of bottom half of cake with jelly; cover with cut side of top. Press almonds and citron randomly into top of cake.

Transfer cake to a trifle or other decorative bowl; pour wine evenly over prepared cake. Cover and refrigerate overnight.

Combine ½ cup sugar and 3 cups milk in top of a double boiler. Place over boiling water, stirring until sugar dissolves.

Combine remaining ¼ cup sugar, 1 cup milk, eggs, flour, and soda in a medium mixing bowl. Gradually add to milk mixture in top of double boiler, stirring constantly. Cook over boiling water, stirring constantly, 20 minutes or until mixture thickens and coats a metal spoon. Stir in vanilla. Remove from heat, and cool.

Pour custard over prepared cake in bowl. Chill thoroughly before serving. Yield: 8 servings.

Trifle is one of the best-loved of the English "puddings." It can be as easy as sliced sponge cake with cream, fruit, and wine. We may substitute angel cake for sponge, as in this menu. For ceremonial use, trifle may contain lady-fingers, good sherry (Irish whiskey for Irish trifle), rich custard, whipped cream, and fruit, fresh or preserved. It may appear in a footed "trifle" dish made for the purpose. Trifle made with red wine was once known as Cardinal Pudding.

TRADITIONAL THANKSGIVING DINNER

Thanksgiving dinner should be direct from the land, according to *The Delineator*, a magazine popular early this century. We should put aside "hothouse ingredients and the charms of foreign cookery" and stick to native, seasonal materials. "All foods should be placed on the table at the start of the meal," the article continues, "to emphasize the bountifulness of the holiday and to allow the cook to enjoy eating without having to rise frequently to bring on another course." This advice, for traditionalists, has not been improved upon. Our golden bird keeps company with an unusually stylish cranberry mold, rich-rich macaroni and cheese, and brussels sprouts in a sauce that's good enough to drink. Go heavy or light for dessert, with a choice between English-style plum pudding and calorie-conscious sherbet.

CRANBERRY-CUMBERLAND SAUCE
ROAST TURKEY WITH OYSTER STUFFING
FRENCH BREAD
CAULIFLOWER À LA VINAIGRETTE
BRUSSELS SPROUTS WITH MAÎTRE D'HÔTEL SAUCE
MACARONI AU GRATIN
PLUM PUDDING
PINEAPPLE SHERBET

Serves 8 to 12

A Thanksgiving Among Their Descendants. *Engraving by W.S.L. Jewett from* Harper's Weekly.

Cherubs serve Thanksgiving dinner. Late 1800s stove ad card.

CRANBERRY-CUMBERLAND SAUCE

Peel of 1 orange, cut into
  ¼-inch-wide strips
⅔ cup fresh orange juice
½ cup red currant jelly
⅓ cup port wine
2 (3-inch) sticks cinnamon
¼ teaspoon ground allspice
2 cups fresh cranberries
1½ cups sugar

Place orange peel in a small saucepan with water to cover; bring to a boil. Reduce heat, and simmer 5 minutes. Drain well, and set aside.

Combine orange juice, jelly, wine, cinnamon, and allspice in a small saucepan. Bring mixture to a boil; reduce heat, and simmer 5 minutes. Discard cinnamon. Add cranberries, and cook over medium heat 5 minutes or until cranberry skins pop, stirring occasionally. Stir in sugar; cook over medium heat 3 minutes or until sugar dissolves. Remove from heat, and chill thoroughly.

Transfer to a serving container, and serve with turkey. Yield: 2½ cups.

ROAST TURKEY WITH OYSTER STUFFING

6 cups cubed French
  bread
2 cups crumbled
  cornbread
3 eggs, beaten
½ cup milk
¼ cup butter or margarine,
  melted
¼ cup chopped onion
1½ teaspoons salt,
  divided
1 teaspoon pepper, divided
1 (12-ounce) container fresh
  Select oysters, drained
  and chopped
1 (12- to 13-pound) turkey
¼ cup vegetable oil
¼ teaspoon onion salt
¼ teaspoon garlic salt
1 cup water

Combine bread cubes, cornbread, eggs, milk, butter, onion, 1 teaspoon salt, and ½ teaspoon pepper in a large mixing bowl; mix well. Stir in oysters.

Remove giblets and neck from turkey; reserve for other uses. Rinse turkey thoroughly with cold water; pat dry.

Stuff oyster dressing into cavity of turkey; close with skewers.

Tie ends of legs to tail with string or tuck them under band of skin at tail. Lift wingtips up and over back, tucking under bird securely.

Brush turkey with oil. Combine remaining salt, pepper, onion salt, and garlic salt; sprinkle mixture over surface of turkey. Place turkey, breast side up, in a covered roaster; pour water in bottom of pan. Cover and bake at 350° for 2½ to 3 hours or until drumsticks are easy to move, basting frequently with pan drippings.

Transfer turkey to a serving platter. Let stand at least 15 minutes before carving. Yield: 8 to 12 servings.

Note: Leftover turkey may be refrigerated for later use.

FRENCH BREAD

1 package dry yeast
1½ cups warm water (105° to
  115°), divided
1 tablespoon sugar
1½ teaspoons salt
1 tablespoon shortening
4 cups all-purpose flour
Yellow cornmeal
1 egg white, slightly beaten
1 tablespoon water
Sesame seeds

Combine yeast and ½ cup warm water in a small mixing bowl. Let stand 5 minutes.

Combine remaining warm water, sugar, and salt in a large mixing bowl; stir until sugar dissolves. Add shortening and yeast mixture, mixing well. Gradually add flour, stirring until dough leaves sides of bowl. Let rest 10 minutes.

Work through dough with a large spoon for 1 minute; repeat procedure 4 additional times at 10 minute intervals. (Cover bowl during intervals.)

Turn dough out onto a lightly floured surface; divide into 2 equal portions. Cover and let rest 10 minutes.

Roll each portion into a 12- x 9-inch rectangle. Roll up each rectangle jellyroll fashion, starting at long end. Pinch seams and ends together to seal. Place loaves, seam side down, in 2 heavily greased baguette pans sprinkled with cornmeal. (Baking sheets may be used in place of baguette pans.)

Cut 6 diagonal slashes, ¾-inch-deep, in top of each loaf. Let rise in a warm place (85°), free from drafts, 1½ hours or until doubled in bulk. Combine egg white and 1 tablespoon water; brush on loaves. Sprinkle with sesame seeds. Bake at 400° for 30 minutes or until loaves sound hollow when tapped. Remove bread from pans or baking sheets immediately. Cool on wire racks. Yield: 2 loaves.

CAULIFLOWER À LA VINAIGRETTE

1 large head cauliflower
Salt and pepper to taste
Vinegar

Wash cauliflower; place cauliflower and water to cover in a small Dutch oven. Cover and bring to a boil. Reduce heat, and simmer 20 minutes or until tender. Drain well.

Transfer cauliflower to a serving plate. Sprinkle with salt and pepper to taste. To serve, break into flowerettes, and dip in vinegar. Yield: 8 to 12 servings.

BRUSSELS SPROUTS WITH MAÎTRE D'HÔTEL SAUCE

48 fresh brussels sprouts
2 tablespoons butter or
  margarine
3 tablespoons all-purpose
  flour
1 cup consommé
1 cup water
1 tablespoon lemon juice
1 tablespoon chopped fresh
  parsley
1 egg yolk

Place brussels sprouts with salt water to barely cover in a small Dutch oven. Bring to a boil; reduce heat, and simmer, uncovered, 20 minutes or until tender. Drain. Place in a serving dish, and keep warm.

Melt butter in a large heavy skillet; gradually add flour, stirring until well blended. Stir in consommé, water, lemon juice, and parsley; cook over medium heat until thickened. Remove from heat, and stir in yolk.

Pour sauce over brussels sprouts, and serve immediately. Yield: 8 to 12 servings.

An early 1900s postcard carried Thanksgiving greetings along with this colorful Turkey gobbler.

MACARONI AU GRATIN

1 cup uncooked elbow
  macaroni
4 eggs, beaten
2 cups milk
½ teaspoon salt
¼ teaspoon pepper
4 cups (1 pound) shredded
  New York sharp Cheddar
  cheese

Cook macaroni according to package directions, omitting salt; drain well. Combine cooked macaroni, eggs, milk, salt, and pepper in a large mixing bowl; stir well. Spoon half of macaroni mixture into a greased 2½-quart shallow baking dish. Sprinkle with half of cheese. Repeat layers with remaining macaroni mixture and cheese, ending with cheese.

Bake at 300° for 30 minutes; increase temperature to 400°, and bake an additional 10 minutes or until lightly browned. Yield: 8 to 12 servings.

Hot Plum Pudding served with Sherried Hard Sauce provides a truly grand finale for a Thanksgiving dinner.

Photograph by John O'Hagan

PLUM PUDDING

1 cup sugar
¾ cup all-purpose flour
½ cup fine, dry breadcrumbs
1½ teaspoons ground
  cinnamon
¼ teaspoon ground cloves
⅛ teaspoon ground mace
1½ cups raisins
1½ cups currants
¾ cup finely chopped citron
1 cup finely chopped almonds
3 eggs, beaten
½ cup grape juice
2 tablespoons lemon juice
¾ cup finely chopped beef
  suet
Sherried hard sauce

Combine first 6 ingredients in a large mixing bowl. Stir in raisins, currants, citron, and almonds; mix well.

Combine eggs, grape juice, and lemon juice. Add to dry mixture; stir in suet. Spoon mixture into a well-greased 2-quart pudding mold; cover tightly.

Place mold on rack in a large deep kettle with enough boiling water to come halfway up mold. Cover kettle; steam pudding 3 hours in boiling water, replacing water as needed. Unmold and serve hot with Sherried Hard Sauce. Refrigerate leftover pudding. Yield: 8 to 12 servings.

Sherried Hard Sauce:

½ cup butter, softened
1 cup sifted powdered sugar
2 tablespoons sherry

Combine butter and sugar; beat until smooth. Add sherry, and beat until fluffy. Chill. Yield: ¾ cup.

PINEAPPLE SHERBET

1 (20-ounce) can crushed
  pineapple, undrained
3 cups sugar
½ cup lemon juice
2 envelopes unflavored
  gelatin
5 cups milk
4 egg whites

Drain pineapple, reserving ½ cup juice. Combine pineapple, sugar, and lemon juice in a large mixing bowl. Set aside.

Dissolve gelatin in pineapple juice in a small saucepan. Bring to a boil, stirring constantly. Remove from heat; stir softened gelatin into pineapple mixture. Cool slightly. Gradually add milk, stirring constantly. Chill.

Beat egg whites (at room temperature) until stiff peaks form. Fold into pineapple mixture.

Pour mixture into freezer can of a 1-gallon hand-turned or electric freezer. Freeze according to manufacturer's instructions. Let ripen at least 1 hour before serving. Yield: 1 gallon.

THANKSGIVING TEA PARTY

In Dickensian England, tea was not just a sip and a snack: It was a ceremony. The lady of the house gathered her family at the fireside and calmly made sure they had nourishment enough to carry them until dinnertime. Tea emerged at last as a popular way of entertaining friends. Just a generation or two ago, the tea dance given at home or in a hotel was considered a splendid affair. Southerners know that a tea is more than a dry cocktail party; it is a moment away from the spinning world. Let's give a tea during the festive Thanksgiving weekend. An Englishman would compliment our "English Biscuits" as scones and consider our cookies "smashing" biscuits.

 ENGLISH BISCUITS WITH CINNAMON BUTTER
NOISETTE SANDWICHES
HIGHLAND COOKIES
LITTLE FANCY CAKES
HOT TEA * HOT CHOCOLATE

Serves 12

Teatime in the 1890s was a time for relaxing with friends and family.

ENGLISH BISCUITS WITH CINNAMON BUTTER

4 cups all-purpose flour
2 tablespoons baking powder
2 tablespoons sugar
1 teaspoon salt
1 cup shortening
2 eggs
1⅓ cups milk
Cinnamon Butter

Combine flour, baking powder, sugar, and salt in a large mixing bowl; stir well. Cut in shortening with a pastry blender until mixture resembles coarse meal. Combine eggs and milk; add to flour mixture, stirring until dry ingredients are moistened.

Turn dough out onto a lightly floured surface; knead lightly 20 times. Roll dough to ¾-inch thickness; cut with a 2-inch biscuit cutter. Place biscuits on ungreased baking sheets. Bake at 450° for 10 minutes or until lightly browned. Serve biscuits hot with Cinnamon Butter. Yield: 2 dozen.

Cinnamon Butter:

1 cup unsalted butter, softened
2 tablespoons sifted powdered sugar
½ teaspoon ground cinnamon

Combine all ingredients in a small mixing bowl; beat well. Yield: about 1 cup.

NOISETTE SANDWICHES

32 slices white bread
2 (3-ounce) packages cream cheese, softened
½ cup ground pecans
2 tablespoons honey
Mint jelly
Guava jelly

Cut 16 slices bread into 2½-inch rounds; set aside. Cut remaining slices with a 2½-inch doughnut cutter; discard centers, and set "doughnuts" aside.

Combine cream cheese, pecans, and honey, beating well. Spread mixture on bread rounds; top with "doughnuts" to form a sandwich. Spoon a small amount of mint jelly into center of 8 sandwiches; spoon guava jelly into center of remaining sandwiches. Yield: 16 appetizer sandwiches.

HIGHLAND COOKIES

1 cup butter, softened
½ cup whipping cream
1¾ cups all-purpose flour
Sifted powdered sugar

Cream butter in a medium mixing bowl; gradually add whipping cream, beating well. Add flour, beating until smooth (dough will be sticky). Divide dough in half; wrap in waxed paper, and chill overnight.

Roll half of dough to ¼-inch thickness on a lightly floured surface; keep remaining dough chilled. Cut dough with assorted shaped cookie cutters; dredge in powdered sugar. Place cookies on lightly greased baking sheets.

Bake at 350° for 15 minutes or until lightly browned. Remove to wire racks to cool.

Repeat procedure with remaining dough. Sprinkle cookies with powdered sugar. Yield: about 3 dozen.

LITTLE FANCY CAKES

½ cup butter or margarine, softened
¼ cup shortening
1½ cups sugar
3 eggs
½ teaspoon vanilla extract
½ teaspoon almond extract
1½ cups cake flour
¼ teaspoon baking powder
½ cup milk
Frosting (recipe follows)

Combine first 3 ingredients in a large mixing bowl, beating well. Add eggs, one at a time, beating well after each addition. Stir in flavorings.

Combine flour and baking powder; add to creamed mixture, beating well. Gradually add milk, beating until smooth.

Pour batter into a greased and floured 13- x 9- x 2-inch baking pan. Bake at 350° for 35 minutes or until a wooden pick inserted in center comes out clean. Cool in pan 10 minutes; remove cake from pan, and allow to cool on wire racks.

Cut cake into small, assorted shapes. Spread top and sides of cakes with frosting. Any leftover frosting may be tinted with food coloring and piped onto cakes with pastry bag, if desired. Yield: about 2 dozen.

Frosting:

2 tablespoons butter or margarine, softened
2 tablespoons shortening
¼ teaspoon salt
3 cups sifted powdered sugar
5 to 6 tablespoons whipping cream

Combine butter, shortening, and salt in a medium mixing bowl; beat well. Add sugar to creamed mixture alternately with cream, beginning and ending with sugar. Beat until smooth. Yield: about 2 cups.

Teatime treats (clockwise from front): Highland Cookies, Noisette Sandwiches, Little Fancy Cakes, and English Biscuits with Cinnamon Butter.

GERMAN-STYLE
CHRISTMAS EVE SUPPER

It was the Germans who brought the custom of the decorated Christmas tree . . . and more . . . to Texas. For their children, they made the holiday one of mystical enchantment with deep religious undertones. To give visitors a glimpse of an authentic turn-of-the-century Christmas Eve, the Sauer-Beckman Living History Farm in the Texas Hill Country has re-created this German-style family gathering: A Texas cedar tree decorated with candles, homemade cookies, and nuts wrapped in colorful bits of paper was kept in a closed-off room until after Christmas Eve supper. Supper was simple then, like the menu below. When the tree room was opened, children ran to the lighted tree in the darkened room to find what Kris Kringle had brought. Gifts were not wrapped; in good times there were oranges and apples.

ASSORTED GERMAN SAUSAGES
SLICED BEEF JERKY
HOMEMADE YEAST LOAVES
COOKED CHEESE
CHRISTMAS COOKIES
LEMON COOKIES
LEBKUCHEN
PFEFFERNÜSSE

Serves 8

Santa prepares to deliver
a tree in all its trimmings.
1900s Christmas card.

SLICED BEEF JERKY

1 (3-pound) sirloin roast
⅓ cup Worcestershire sauce
¼ cup soy sauce
1 teaspoon onion powder
1 teaspoon garlic powder
½ teaspoon pepper
½ teaspoon liquid smoke

Cut roast into 6- x ½- x ¼-inch strips across the grain. Combine remaining ingredients, and pour over beef strips; toss to coat evenly. Chill 1 hour.

Cover bottom wire rack in oven with aluminum foil. Hang beef strips on top wire rack 1 inch apart.

Bake at 175° (with door ajar) 4 hours or until jerky is bendable but not brittle. Yield: 1 pound.

Note: Partially freeze meat for easier slicing. Store jerky in an airtight container.

HOMEMADE YEAST LOAVES

2 packages dry yeast
¼ cup warm water (105° to 115°)
1 cup scalded milk
1 cup warm water (105° to 115°)
2 tablespoons sugar
1½ tablespoons butter or margarine
1½ tablespoons shortening
2½ teaspoons salt
6 to 6½ cups all-purpose flour
Butter or margarine, melted

Dissolve yeast in ¼ cup warm water, stirring well; let stand 10 minutes or until bubbly.

Let milk cool to 105° to 115° in a large bowl; add warm water, sugar, 1½ tablespoons butter, shortening, and salt, stirring well. Add dissolved yeast; stir well. Stir in enough flour to make a soft dough. Cover and let stand 15 minutes.

Turn dough out onto a floured surface, and knead 10 minutes or until smooth and elastic. Place dough in a greased bowl, turning to grease top. Cover and let rise in a warm place (85°), free from drafts, 1 hour or until doubled in bulk.

Punch dough down; turn out onto a lightly floured surface. Divide dough in half, shaping each into a smooth ball. Cover; let rest 10 minutes.

Shape each portion into a loaf; place in 2 greased 9- x 5- x 3-inch loafpans. Brush tops of loaves with butter. Cover; repeat rising procedure 45 minutes or until doubled in bulk. Bake at 450° for 10 minutes; reduce heat to 350°. Bake 30 minutes or until loaves sound hollow when tapped. Remove from pans immediately; cool on wire racks. Yield: 2 loaves.

COOKED CHEESE

2 cups cottage cheese
2 tablespoons all-purpose flour
½ teaspoon baking soda
½ teaspoon salt
½ cup whipping cream
¼ cup butter

Combine cottage cheese, flour, baking soda, and salt in a large mixing bowl. Let cottage cheese mixture sit at room temperature for 2 hours or until mixture is bubbly.

Combine cottage cheese mixture, whipping cream, and butter in a 9-inch cast-iron skillet. Cook over low heat, stirring frequently, 25 minutes or until thickened. Remove from heat, and cool slightly. Serve with fresh homemade breads or chill and serve with crackers. Yield: about 3 cups.

CHRISTMAS COOKIES

½ cup butter, softened
1 cup plus 2½ tablespoons firmly packed brown sugar
3 eggs
¼ teaspoon baking soda
2 tablespoons water
4 to 4¼ cups all-purpose flour
½ teaspoon baking powder
2¼ teaspoons ground cinnamon
¾ teaspoon ground allspice
½ teaspoon ground cloves
½ teaspoon ground cardamom

Cream butter; gradually add sugar, beating well. Add eggs, one at a time, beating well after each addition. Dissolve soda in water; add to creamed mixture, mixing well. Combine remaining ingredients; add to creamed mixture, mixing well. Divide dough in half; wrap in waxed paper, and chill at least 1 hour.

Roll half of dough to ⅛-inch thickness on a lightly floured surface; keep remaining dough chilled. Cut dough with assorted cookie cutters. Bake on lightly greased baking sheets at 350° for 10 minutes. Cool on wire racks. Yield: about 6 dozen.

"God bless the children." Christmas card, c.1900.

LEMON COOKIES

1 cup butter, softened
1 cup sugar
6 egg yolks, slightly beaten
2 teaspoons grated lemon rind
3½ cups all-purpose flour
3 egg yolks, beaten
1 cup sugar
1 cup finely chopped pecans
2 tablespoons ground cinnamon

Cream butter; gradually add 1 cup sugar, beating until light and fluffy. Add 6 yolks and lemon rind; beat well. Gradually add flour to creamed mixture, and mix well.

Turn dough out onto a lightly floured surface. Roll to ¼-inch thickness, and cut with assorted 2-inch cookie cutters. Place cookies on lightly greased baking sheets. Brush tops of cookies with 3 egg yolks. Combine 1 cup sugar, pecans, and cinnamon; sprinkle over cookies. Bake at 350° for 15 minutes. Cool cookies on wire racks. Yield: about 3½ dozen.

Christmas Cookies (front),
Lemon Cookies (left),
Lebkuchen (right), and
Pfeffernüsse (rear).

LEBKUCHEN

3 cups sugar
1½ cups water
1 cup butter or margarine
1½ teaspoons ground
  cinnamon
1½ teaspoons ground nutmeg
1½ teaspoons ground cloves
½ teaspoon baking soda
2 tablespoons warm water
5¼ cups all-purpose flour
1 teaspoon baking powder

Combine sugar, water, and
butter in a large Dutch oven;
bring to a boil. Remove from
heat. Add cinnamon, nutmeg,
and cloves; stir well, and cool.
Dissolve soda in warm water.
Add flour, baking powder, and
dissolved soda to cooled spice
mixture; mix well.
Shape dough into three 10-
inch-long rolls; wrap in waxed
paper, and refrigerate 8 days.
Dough will be sticky.
Unwrap roll, and cut into ¼-
inch slices. Place cookies on
lightly greased baking sheets.
Bake at 350° for 12 minutes.
Cool on wire racks. Yield: about
7½ dozen.
Note: For a uniform cookie
slice, use a piece of string
wrapped around the cookie roll.
Wrap the string around the bottom of the roll and criss-cross
the ends at the top. Pull string
away from roll to slice.
This results in a more uniform cookie slice which doesn't
affect the shape of the remaining roll.

PFEFFERNÜSSE

¼ cup plus 2 tablespoons
  butter or margarine,
  softened
¾ cup sugar
1 egg
¼ cup light corn syrup
1½ tablespoons buttermilk
1¾ cups all-purpose flour
1 teaspoon baking powder
¼ teaspoon baking soda
½ teaspoon ground cinnamon
¼ teaspoon ground cardamom
¼ teaspoon ground ginger
¼ teaspoon ground nutmeg
¼ teaspoon ground cloves
¼ teaspoon ground mace
⅛ teaspoon anise extract

Cream softened butter in a
medium mixing bowl; add
sugar, egg, corn syrup, and buttermilk, beating well. Combine
flour, baking powder, soda, and
spices; gradually add flour mixture to creamed mixture, beating well. Add anise extract, and
mix well.
Drop dough by heaping teaspoonfuls onto well-greased
baking sheets. Bake at 375° for
10 minutes or until lightly
browned. Cool slightly on baking sheets; transfer to wire
racks and cool completely. Yield:
about 4 dozen.

OKLAHOMA TERRITORY
CHRISTMAS DINNER

Christmas came to the Indian and Oklahoma Territories with the first missionaries in the 1820s, decades before the land rush of the late 1800s. And it was duly celebrated despite all difficulties. The varied terrains of the area had much to do with the tree selection. In the central plains, blackjack oak would be the "choice," unless men rode for miles for a native cedar.

The oak or a leafless limb could be made into an enchanting tree for the children by covering each branch in cotton to make it snowy; popcorn strings and homemade cookies were added. Men who chewed tobacco saved the tinfoil wrapping from the cut plug and used it for "icicles" or to wrap nuts for ornaments. Dinner was less of a problem: Game birds were there for the taking.

HOLIDAY BAKED QUAIL
WILD RICE
FRESH PLUM JELLY
GREEN PEAS
MUSHROOM-ONION CUSTARD
BACON BISCUITS
PERSIMMON PUDDING

Serves 6

Homesteaders vie for space on the Cherokee Strip, Oklahoma land rush, 1893.

HOLIDAY BAKED QUAIL

2 cups all-purpose
  flour
2 teaspoons salt
1 teaspoon pepper
12 quail, cleaned
½ cup shortening

Combine flour, salt, and pepper in a medium mixing bowl; stir well. Dredge each cleaned quail in flour mixture.

Melt shortening in a large cast-iron skillet; add quail, and brown on both sides. Remove from skillet, and drain well on paper towels.

Transfer quail to a lightly greased 2-quart casserole. Cover and bake at 350° for 25 minutes or until quail is tender. Serve quail over Wild Rice. Yield: 6 servings.

WILD RICE

1 (6-ounce) package long
  grain and wild rice mix
1 (6-ounce) can sliced
  mushrooms, undrained
1 small onion, chopped
½ cup chopped celery
¼ cup chopped green pepper
¼ cup chopped blanched
  almonds
¼ cup plus 2 tablespoons
  butter or margarine

Cook rice according to package directions. Set aside.

Sauté mushrooms and liquid, onion, celery, green pepper, and almonds in butter in a large skillet 15 minutes or until liquid is absorbed. Stir in rice mixture. Spoon mixture into a 1½-quart casserole. Cover and bake at 350° for 30 minutes. Yield: 6 servings.

FRESH PLUM JELLY

3 pounds fresh plums,
  stemmed
6 cups water
3⅓ cups sugar

Combine plums and water in a large Dutch oven; bring to a boil. Reduce heat; cover and simmer 20 to 25 minutes. Remove seeds from plums; return to cooking liquid, and mash slightly. Strain plum mixture through a jelly bag or 4 layers of cheesecloth, reserving 5 cups juice. Discard pulp.

Combine 5 cups juice and sugar in a large Dutch oven; bring to a rolling boil, stirring frequently. Boil until mixture reaches 220° on candy thermometer, stirring frequently. Remove from heat, and skim off foam with a metal spoon.

Quickly pour jelly into hot, sterilized jars, leaving ½-inch headspace. Cover at once with metal lids, and screw bands tight. Yield: about 3 half pints.

GREEN PEAS

1 cup water
2 beef-flavored bouillon
  cubes
2 (10-ounce) packages frozen
  green peas
¼ cup butter or margarine,
  melted
1½ teaspoons sugar
1 teaspoon salt
¼ teaspoon pepper

Combine water and bouillon cubes in a saucepan. Bring to a boil; stir until bouillon cubes dissolve. Add peas. Reduce heat; cover and simmer 5 minutes or until peas are tender. Drain; add butter, sugar, salt, and pepper, stirring gently until well combined. Serve immediately. Yield: 6 servings.

Holiday Baked Quail, Oklahoma style, on Wild Rice, served with Green Peas and Fresh Plum Jelly.

MUSHROOM-ONION CUSTARD

½ cup butter or margarine, divided
1½ cups coarsely crushed cracker crumbs
½ teaspoon curry powder
½ pound fresh mushrooms, sliced
1 medium-size Spanish onion, thinly sliced
2 cups (8 ounces) shredded sharp Cheddar cheese
1½ cups milk, scalded
3 eggs, beaten
½ teaspoon salt
Dash of red pepper

Melt ¼ cup butter; add cracker crumbs and curry powder, stirring well. Press cracker mixture into bottom of a 10- x 6- x 2-inch baking dish. Set aside.

Sauté mushrooms and onion in remaining butter in a large skillet 5 minutes or until tender. Remove from heat. Stir in remaining ingredients.

Spoon mixture into prepared dish. Bake at 350° for 30 minutes. Yield: 6 servings.

BACON BISCUITS

1½ cups all-purpose flour
2½ teaspoons baking powder
¼ teaspoon salt
½ cup shortening
1 cup (4 ounces) shredded sharp Cheddar cheese
½ cup cooked, crumbled bacon
¼ cup chopped onion
½ cup milk

Combine flour, baking powder, and salt; stir well. Cut in shortening until mixture resembles coarse meal. Stir in cheese, bacon, and onion. Add milk, stirring until ingredients are moistened.

Turn dough out onto a heavily floured surface, and lightly knead 4 to 5 times.

Roll dough into a 10- x 7-inch rectangle; cut into 3- x 1-inch rectangles. Place on greased baking sheets. Bake at 425° for 12 minutes or until lightly browned. Yield: about 2 dozen.

Ramshackle frontier hotel borrows a well-known name.

PERSIMMON PUDDING

2 eggs
1 cup persimmon pulp
1 cup sugar
1 cup all-purpose flour
1 teaspoon ground cinnamon
1 teaspoon ground nutmeg
Pinch of salt
1 teaspoon baking soda
¼ cup buttermilk
1 teaspoon vanilla extract
1 cup chopped pecans
Hard sauce (recipe follows)

Beat eggs until light and frothy in a large mixing bowl. Add persimmon and sugar, beating well. Combine flour, cinnamon, nutmeg, and salt; stir well. Add to egg mixture, beating well. Dissolve soda in buttermilk; add to pudding mixture. Stir in vanilla and pecans.

Pour batter into a well-greased 1½-quart pudding mold, and cover tightly with lid. Place mold on rack in a large kettle; add boiling water, filling kettle half full. Bring to a boil. Reduce heat; cover and simmer 2 hours.

Remove mold from kettle; remove lid from mold to allow steam to escape. Cool 10 minutes. Loosen pudding from sides of mold, and invert onto a serving dish. Serve warm with hard sauce. Yield: 6 servings.

Hard Sauce:

½ cup butter or margarine, softened
½ cup sifted powdered sugar
2 tablespoons brandy
Dash of ground nutmeg

Combine butter and powdered sugar, beating until smooth. Gradually add brandy and nutmeg; beat until fluffy. Yield: about ½ cup.

Note: Persimmon Pudding may be flamed by quickly heating 2 tablespoons brandy in a small saucepan to just warm. Pour over pudding, and ignite with a long match. Present at the table while still flaming. When flames die down, slice and serve warm with hard sauce.

CHRISTMAS EGGNOG
AT HOPE FARM

Hope Farm in Natchez had its beginnings around 1775 and today is one of the most beautiful restorations to be toured on the Natchez Pilgrimage. The present owners, the J. Balfour Millers, are known for their hospitality and each year give a Christmas morning eggnog party for their friends. The Hope Farm eggnog recipe is similar to another antebellum version from Louisiana of which Bernard Bares wrote this lyrical passage: "It was truly a nectar of Romance. Charming and gracious ladies, bedecked in jewels, attired in silks and satins, and their gentlemen escorts, raised silver cups of it, to toast a way-of-life which they believed would never end. . . ."

CHRISTMAS EGGNOG * HOT CHOCOLATE
JINGLE BREAD COFFEE CAKE

Serves 8 to 10

CHRISTMAS EGGNOG

18 eggs, separated
2 cups sugar
1 (750 ml) bottle whiskey
2 quarts whipping cream
Ground nutmeg

Beat egg yolks in a large bowl at medium speed of an electric mixer until thick and lemon colored. Gradually add sugar, beating constantly. Slowly add whiskey, beating constantly. Beat in whipping cream.

Beat egg whites (at room temperature) until stiff. Fold egg whites into cream mixture. Chill. Sprinkle with nutmeg before serving. Yield: 1½ gallons.

All that's needed for a party: Jingle Bread Coffee Cake accompanied by the richly potent Hope Farm Christmas Eggnog.

Photograph by John O'Hagan

The dining room of Hope Farm has been the scene for many a Christmas festivity.

JINGLE BREAD COFFEE CAKE

2 packages dry yeast
½ cup warm water (105°
  to 115°)
⅓ cup sugar
2 teaspoons salt
¼ cup shortening, melted
1 cup warm buttermilk
  (105° to 115°)
2 eggs, beaten
4½ cups all-purpose flour
½ cup honey
½ cup sugar
2 tablespoons grated
  lemon rind
2 tablespoons grated
  orange rind
2 tablespoons orange juice
1 teaspoon ground cinnamon
¾ cup chopped pecans
¾ cup chopped raisins

Dissolve yeast in warm water; let stand 5 minutes.

Combine ⅓ cup sugar, salt, shortening, and buttermilk in a large bowl. Stir in dissolved yeast and eggs. Gradually add flour, stirring until a soft dough is formed. Place in a well-greased bowl, turning to grease top. Cover and let rise in a warm place (85°), free from drafts, 2 hours or until doubled in bulk.

Punch dough down. Turn dough out onto a lightly floured surface, and roll into an 18-inch square.

Combine remaining ingredients; spread mixture over square. Roll up jellyroll fashion; moisten edges, and pinch to seal. Cut roll into 1-inch-thick slices. Place slices, cut side down, in layers in a well-greased 10-inch tube pan.

Cover and let rise in a warm place (85°), free from drafts, 1 hour or until doubled in bulk. Bake at 350° for 50 minutes or until golden brown. Cut into wedges to serve. Yield: one 10-inch coffee cake.

MIDDLETON PLACE
CHRISTMAS DINNER

The opulence of a Southern colonial plantation Christmas dinner is beyond modern imagining. At 4 p.m., according to one written account, twenty people sat down to (just to mention the meats) beef, venison, ham, ducks, turkey, chicken, oyster pie, and pork. The locale could have been Middleton Place, twenty miles from Charleston, South Carolina, where such meals were the norm. Henry Middleton built the main house facing the Ashley River in 1741; two separate wings or "flankers" were added later, as well as one of the finest classical gardens in the Western World. Restored Middleton Place, a National Historic Landmark, is open to the public and is managed by a descendant of Henry Middleton. Our menu may be only a shadow of plantation feasting, but it is grand by today's standards.

OYSTER STEW
ROAST TURKEY WITH RICE-PECAN STUFFING
GINGER CARROTS
GREEN BEANS ITALIENNE
CRANBERRY-ORANGE RELISH
BUTTERMILK BISCUITS
JAPANESE FRUIT CAKE
AMBROSIA

Serves 10

OYSTER STEW

1½ cups chopped onion
2 stalks celery, sliced
2 cloves garlic, minced
2 sprigs fresh parsley, chopped
¼ teaspoon dried whole thyme
¼ cup plus 2 tablespoons butter or margarine
4½ cups half-and-half
2 (12-ounce) containers fresh Select oysters, undrained
¼ cup plus 2 tablespoons golden sherry
¾ teaspoon salt
¼ teaspoon pepper
¼ teaspoon Worcestershire sauce
⅛ teaspoon hot sauce

Sauté onion, celery, garlic, parsley, and thyme in butter in a large Dutch oven until vegetables are tender. Gradually add half-and-half, stirring constantly.

Drain oysters, reserving liquid. Add liquid to vegetable mixture; heat thoroughly without boiling. Stir in oysters, sherry, salt, pepper, Worcestershire sauce, and hot sauce. Continue cooking over low heat, stirring constantly, until mixture is heated and oyster edges curl. Serve warm. Yield: 10 cups.

Middleton Place

Middleton Place was the site of the formal British surrender, 1781. Here, sheep clip grass before the lone survivor of three original buildings.

umptuous Christmas dinner photographed at Middleton Place.

Aerial view of Middleton Place on the Ashley River near Charleston.

ROAST TURKEY WITH RICE-PECAN STUFFING

2 (6-ounce) packages long grain and wild rice mix
1½ cups chopped green onion
1½ cups chopped celery
1½ cups sliced fresh mushrooms
1 tablespoon chopped fresh parsley
½ cup butter or margarine
1½ cups chopped pecans, toasted
1 teaspoon salt
¾ teaspoon rubbed sage
¾ teaspoon dried whole thyme
¼ teaspoon pepper
1 (12- to 14-pound) turkey
½ cup butter or margarine, melted and divided

Cook rice according to package directions; set aside.

Sauté green onion, celery, mushrooms, and parsley in ½ cup butter until tender. Combine sautéed vegetables, rice, pecans, salt, sage, thyme, and pepper; mix well. Set aside.

Remove giblets and neck from turkey; reserve for other uses. Rinse turkey thoroughly with cold water; pat dry.

Stuff dressing into cavity of turkey; close with skewers. Place remaining stuffing in a greased 2-quart casserole. Cover and refrigerate. Tie ends of legs to tail with string or tuck them under band of skin at tail. Lift wingtips up and over back, tucking under bird securely.

Brush entire bird with ¼ cup melted butter; place breast side up on a rack in a roasting pan. Insert meat thermometer in breast or meaty part of thigh, making sure it does not touch bone. Bake turkey at 325° for 3 hours, basting frequently with remaining butter. Cut string or band of skin holding drumstick ends to tail. Bake reserved stuffing and turkey an additional 30 minutes or until drumsticks are easy to move and meat thermometer registers 185°.

Remove stuffing and turkey from oven. Transfer turkey to a serving platter. Let stand 15 minutes before serving. Yield: 10 servings.

Note: Leftover turkey may be refrigerated for later use.

Middleton Place once comprised about 50,000 acres, and rice was the principal crop. The garden, with its parterre, terraces, and Butterfly Lakes, was designed for controlling the flooding of water onto the riceland. The main house and north flanker were torched by Union soldiers in 1865 and finished off by the earthquake of 1886. This aerial view shows the remaining south wing sitting to the right of the garden's central axis.

GINGER CARROTS

20 medium carrots, scraped and cut into ¼-inch slices
½ cup butter or margarine, melted
½ cup honey
1 teaspoon salt
½ teaspoon ground cinnamon
½ teaspoon ground ginger

Cook carrots in a small amount of boiling water 20 minutes or until crisp-tender; drain.

Combine carrots, butter, honey, salt, cinnamon, and ginger in a medium saucepan. Cook over medium heat, stirring gently, until carrots are well coated and thoroughly heated. Yield: 10 servings.

GREEN BEANS ITALIENNE

1 cup chopped onion
¼ cup plus 2 tablespoons butter or margarine
3 (14½-ounce) cans whole tomatoes, undrained and quartered
3 (16-ounce) cans cut green beans, drained
1 teaspoon salt
¾ teaspoon ground oregano
¾ teaspoon dried whole basil
¼ teaspoon pepper

Sauté onion in butter in a large saucepan over low heat until tender. Add remaining ingredients; simmer 15 minutes or until thoroughly heated. Yield: 10 servings.

A watercolor by Alice Ravenal Huger Smith (1876-1958) of South Carolina rice growing.

Carolina Art Association/Gibbes Art Gallery, Charleston, South Carolina

Portrait of Arthur and Mary Middleton with son Henry: oil on canvas, 1771, by Benjamin West, a well-known portrait artist of that period.

CRANBERRY-ORANGE RELISH

5 cups fresh cranberries
2 cups sugar
1 cup orange juice
½ cup finely chopped orange rind
½ teaspoon ground nutmeg
½ teaspoon ground cardamom

Combine cranberries, sugar, orange juice, rind, nutmeg, and cardamom in a heavy saucepan; stir well. Bring to a boil. Reduce heat, and simmer 10 minutes or until cranberry skins pop, stirring occasionally. Remove from heat; cool. Transfer to a serving bowl, and chill thoroughly. Yield: 4 cups.

BUTTERMILK BISCUITS

2 cups all-purpose flour
1 teaspoon baking powder
½ teaspoon baking soda
¾ teaspoon salt
3 tablespoons shortening
1 cup buttermilk

Combine flour, baking powder, soda, and salt; stir well. Cut in shortening with a pastry blender until mixture resembles coarse meal. Gradually add buttermilk, stirring until dry ingredients are moistened.

Turn dough out onto a lightly floured surface, and knead 10 to 12 times. Roll dough to ½-inch thickness; cut with a 2-inch biscuit cutter. Place biscuits on an ungreased baking sheet. Bake at 400° for 10 minutes or until lightly browned. Yield: about 1½ dozen.

Henry Middleton's silver tankard shows details of crest and coat of arms.

JAPANESE FRUIT CAKE

¾ cup shortening
2½ cups sugar, divided
1½ teaspoons vanilla extract
2¼ cups cake flour
1 tablespoon plus 1½
  teaspoons baking powder,
  divided
1½ teaspoons salt, divided
1 cup skim milk
5 egg whites
⅓ cup butter or margarine,
  softened
2 eggs
1¾ cups all-purpose flour
1 teaspoon ground cloves
1 cup milk
½ cup finely chopped pecans,
  toasted
½ cup candied red cherries,
  chopped
¼ cup chopped raisins
Filling (recipe follows)
Frosting (recipe follows)
½ cup chopped pecans,
  toasted (optional)
½ cup red maraschino
  cherries, halved (optional)

Grease and flour three 9-inch round cakepans. Set aside.

Cream shortening; gradually add 1½ cups sugar, beating well. Add vanilla; beat well.

Combine cake flour, 1 tablespoon baking powder, and 1 teaspoon salt; add to creamed mixture alternately with skim milk, beginning and ending with flour mixture.

Beat 5 egg whites (at room temperature) until stiff peaks form. Gently fold into batter.

Spoon batter into 2 prepared cakepans. Bake at 375° for 25 minutes or until a wooden pick inserted in center comes out clean. Cool in pans 10 minutes; remove layers from pans, and let cool completely.

Cream butter; gradually add remaining sugar, beating well. Add 2 eggs, one at a time, beating well after each addition.

Combine 1¾ cups flour, remaining baking powder, salt, and cloves; add to creamed mixture alternately with 1 cup milk, beginning and ending with flour mixture. Fold in ½ cup

pecans, ½ cup chopped cherries, and raisins.

Spoon batter into the one remaining prepared cakepan.

Bake at 350° for 35 minutes or until a wooden pick inserted in center comes out clean. Cool in pan 10 minutes; remove layer from pan, and let cool completely.

Spread filling between layers and on top, placing the dark layer between the two white layers. Spread frosting on sides of cake. Garnish top of cake with ½ cup pecans and cherry halves, if desired. Yield: one 3-layer cake.

Filling:

8 egg yolks, well beaten
3 cups sugar
1 cup golden raisins
6 medium oranges, peeled,
  seeded, and chopped
2 tablespoons butter or
  margarine
1 (8-ounce) can crushed
  pineapple, drained
1 cup grated fresh coconut

Combine egg yolks, sugar, raisins, oranges, and butter in top of a double boiler. Cook over boiling water, stirring occasionally, 30 minutes or until thickened. Add pineapple and coconut; cook an additional 10 minutes, stirring occasionally.

Remove from heat, and cool. Chill filling slightly before

spreading on cake. Yield: filling for one 3-layer cake.

Frosting:

¾ cup sugar
1 egg white
1½ teaspoons light corn
  syrup
Dash of salt
2½ tablespoons cold water
½ teaspoon vanilla extract

Combine sugar, egg white, syrup, and salt in top of a double boiler; add cold water, and beat at low speed of an electric mixer 30 seconds.

Place over boiling water; beat constantly at high speed 7 minutes or until stiff peaks form. Remove from heat. Add vanilla; beat 2 additional minutes or until thick enough to spread. Yield: enough to frost sides of a 3-layer cake.

AMBROSIA

12 medium oranges, peeled
  and sliced crosswise
4 cups shredded fresh
  coconut
2 (6-ounce) jars red
  maraschino cherries,
  drained and cut in half

Combine all ingredients in a large serving bowl. Toss lightly until well mixed. Cover and refrigerate overnight. Yield: 10 servings.

Christmas greeting card, c.1910, depicts winter scene.

PRÓSPERO AÑO NUEVO

Of the many ways in which Southerners usher in the New Year, there could scarcely be a gentler, more affectionate one than the Mexican custom observed by the family of Mariano Martinez, a Dallas restaurateur. As for generations past, the family gathers at the dining room table at midnight on New Year's Eve for a cup of hot chocolate and, for luck, the golden fried pastries called buñuelos. Days ahead of time, Mexican-American mothers, daughters, sisters, and grandmothers make a flurry of telephone calls, pretending to have forgotten the buñuelo recipe. And, as long as they're chatting, it is an ideal time to say, "Próspero Año Nuevo!"

BUÑUELOS
HOT CHOCOLATE

Serves 8

BUÑUELOS

4 cups all-purpose flour
1 teaspoon baking powder
1 teaspoon salt
1 cup milk
2 eggs, beaten
1 tablespoon shortening, melted
Vegetable oil
1 cup sugar
1 teaspoon cinnamon

Combine flour, baking powder, and salt in a large bowl. Combine milk, eggs, and shortening; add to dry ingredients, stirring just until moistened.

Shape dough into 1½-inch balls, and place on a lightly floured surface. Roll each ball into a very thin circle about 6 to 7 inches in diameter.

Heat 1 inch of oil in a large, heavy skillet to 375°. Fry each buñuelo 1 minute on each side or until lightly browned. Drain on paper towels.

Combine sugar and cinnamon; sprinkle over buñuelos. Yield: 2 dozen.

The Mexican Buñuelo is a fried pastry so brittle-crisp and light it fairly melts in the mouth. Be sure to make plenty to serve with Hot Chocolate.

HOT CHOCOLATE

6 (1-ounce) squares
  semisweet chocolate
¼ cup plus 2 tablespoons
  water
2 quarts milk
½ cup sugar

Melt chocolate in water in a saucepan; add milk. Bring to a boil; stir constantly. Remove from heat. Add sugar; beat 5 minutes at medium speed of an electric mixer. Yield: 2 quarts.

Tlaxcalan Indians receiving Cortez in Xaltelolco, Mexico. Drawing by Genaro López, 1892.

GREEK NEW YEAR'S DINNER

January 1 is New Year's Day, but to Southerners of Greek ancestry that fact is almost incidental. It is the Feast Day of St. Basil, a bishop who died on that date in 379 A.D. The feast always includes Vasilopeta, the famous Greek sweet bread. In memory of St. Basil, who gave away loaves of bread with coins baked into them to the poor, a coin is kneaded into each loaf.

When the bread is cut, the slices are "named," the first one for the house, followed by one for each family member and guest. Finding the coin in one's slice promises good fortune for the coming year. This delectable menu is based on St. Basil's Feast Day Dinner. The rolled honey pastries or Diples are fun to make; they really can be rolled up while they fry.

STUFFED GRAPE LEAVES
FRIED CHEESE FLAMBÉ
GRECIAN-STYLE ROAST PORK WITH POTATOES
BLACK-EYED PEA SALAD
SPINACH PIE
GREEK BREAD
VASILOPETA (Greek Sweet Bread)
DIPLES (Rolled Honey Pastry)

Serves 10

STUFFED GRAPE LEAVES

1 (16-ounce) jar grapevine leaves, drained
3 small onions, finely chopped
¾ cup olive oil, divided
1 bunch green onions, finely chopped
¾ cup regular rice, uncooked
½ cup chopped fresh parsley
¼ cup pine nuts
¼ cup water
1 tablespoon lemon juice
1½ teaspoons dried mint leaves
1 teaspoon salt
½ teaspoon pepper
½ teaspoon dried whole dillweed
Fresh parsley stalks
2 cups boiling water
1 tablespoon lemon juice
Salt and pepper to taste
Additional lemon juice
Lemon slices

Scald grapevine leaves in boiling water in a medium saucepan; drain well. Cut large leaves in half and leave small leaves intact. Set aside.

Sauté onion in ¼ cup olive oil in a small Dutch oven until tender. Add green onion, rice, parsley, pine nuts, ¼ cup water, 1 tablespoon lemon juice, mint, 1 teaspoon salt, ½ teaspoon pepper, and dillweed; stir well. Cover and cook over medium-low heat 10 minutes, stirring occasionally. Remove from heat; cool slightly.

Arrange parsley stalks to cover bottom of a 4-quart Dutch oven; set aside.

Spoon about 1 heaping teaspoon of onion mixture into center of each prepared grapevine leaf. Fold edges of leaf around mixture, overlapping edges to secure. Place each stuffed grapevine leaf, seam side down, over parsley stalks in Dutch oven. Pour remaining olive oil, boiling water, and 1 tablespoon lemon juice over top.

Invert a heavy plate over stuffed grapevine leaves to secure stuffed leaves during simmering process. Cover and cook over low heat 45 minutes; add more water, if necessary.

Remove from heat. Transfer stuffed grapevine leaves to a serving platter; add salt and pepper to taste. Sprinkle with additional lemon juice and garnish with lemon slices to serve. Yield: 10 servings.

Spinach Pie, a round of Greek Bread, and Black-Eyed Pea Salad, Greek style.

Two young children dressed up in traditional Greek festival costumes.

FRIED CHEESE FLAMBÉ

1½ pounds Kasseri or Kefalotyri cheese
4 eggs, well beaten
2¼ cups all-purpose flour
1½ cups butter
¼ cup plus 2 tablespoons brandy
¼ cup plus 2 tablespoons lemon juice

Slice cheese into 3- x ½-inch pieces. Dip cheese in egg; dredge in flour, coating thoroughly. Place on waxed paper, and chill 1 hour.

Melt butter in a heavy skillet over medium heat. Fry cheese in butter 10 seconds on each side. Drain on paper towels. Transfer cheese to a serving platter.

Place brandy in a small, long-handled pan; heat just until warm (do not boil). Ignite brandy with a long match, and pour over cheese. When flames die down, sprinkle lemon juice over cheese. Serve immediately. Yield: 10 servings.

GRECIAN-STYLE ROAST PORK WITH POTATOES

1 (4- to 4½-pound) pork loin roast
Juice of 1 lemon
1 teaspoon salt, divided
1 teaspoon ground oregano
½ teaspoon pepper, divided
4 cups water
½ cup Chablis or other dry, white wine
10 medium-size russet potatoes, unpeeled and quartered

Sprinkle surface of roast with lemon juice, ½ teaspoon salt, oregano, and ¼ teaspoon pepper. Place roast, fat side up, in a large roasting pan; insert meat thermometer, if desired.

Bake roast, uncovered, at 450° for 10 minutes. Pour water and wine over roast; reduce heat to 325°, and bake 1 hour and 35 minutes.

Sprinkle potatoes with remaining salt and pepper; arrange potatoes around roast, and bake an additional 1 hour and 20 minutes or until meat thermometer registers 170° and potatoes are tender. Let roast stand 10 minutes before carving. Yield: 10 servings.

BLACK-EYED PEA SALAD

½ cup olive oil
2 tablespoons lemon juice
1 teaspoon ground oregano
¼ teaspoon garlic salt
⅛ teaspoon pepper
3 cups cooked black-eyed peas
1 small onion, chopped
½ cup chopped celery
Lettuce leaves

Combine first 5 ingredients in a small bowl; mix well.

Combine peas, onion, and celery in a large mixing bowl. Pour oil mixture over pea mixture, and toss well. Cover and refrigerate at least 3 hours. Spoon into a lettuce-lined bowl to serve. Yield: 10 servings.

SPINACH PIE

2 bunches green onions, chopped
2 (10-ounce) packages frozen chopped spinach, thawed and drained
1 (16-ounce) carton commercial sour cream
1½ cups cottage cheese
¼ cup crumbled feta cheese
2 tablespoons dried whole dillweed
1 teaspoon salt
½ teaspoon pepper
½ teaspoon cream of wheat
3 eggs, beaten
1½ cups butter or margarine, melted
1 (16-ounce) package frozen filo pastry, thawed

Combine onion and water to cover in a heavy saucepan. Bring to a boil. Reduce heat; simmer 5 minutes or until onion is tender. Drain well.

Combine onion, spinach, sour cream, cottage cheese, feta cheese, dillweed, salt, pepper, cream of wheat, and eggs in a large mixing bowl; stir well.

Brush a 15- x 10- x 1-inch jellyroll pan with butter. Fold one sheet filo in half, and place at short end of pan with fold extending over side of pan. Repeat procedure at other end of pan, and on long sides of pan. Brush all sheets with butter. Place one full sheet on bottom of pan; brush with butter. Repeat procedure with 8 sheets on bottom.

Spread spinach mixture over filo pastry. Fold all ends over spinach mixture. Layer 8 filo sheets on top of spinach mixture, brushing each layer with butter. Trim edges of filo sheets, if necessary.

Score top filo layers into 2½-inch squares using a sharp knife. Sprinkle with a few drops of water. Bake at 350° for 1 hour or until golden brown. Cut into scored squares using a very sharp knife. Serve warm. Yield: 2 dozen.

Note: Spinach pie may be frozen and thawed just prior to baking.

GREEK BREAD

2 packages dry yeast
½ cup plus 1½ teaspoons
   sugar, divided
1 cup warm water (105°
   to 115°)
1¼ cups milk, scalded
2 teaspoons salt
½ cup shortening
¼ cup butter or margarine
3 eggs, beaten
7 cups all-purpose flour,
   divided
1 egg, beaten
¼ cup sesame seeds

Dissolve yeast and 1½ teaspoons sugar in warm water; let stand 5 minutes.

Combine milk, salt, shortening, butter, and remaining sugar in a large bowl; stir until sugar dissolves. Cool to lukewarm (105° to 115°). Add yeast mixture and 3 eggs, stirring well. Add 4 cups flour; beat well.

Stir in remaining flour to make a soft dough. Turn dough out onto a lightly floured surface; knead 5 minutes. Place in a greased bowl, turning to grease top. Cover and let rise in a warm place (85°), free from drafts, 50 minutes or until doubled in bulk.

Punch dough down, and let rest 5 minutes. Divide dough into 3 equal portions. Roll each portion into an 18-inch rope. Shape each rope into a loose coil in three greased 8-inch round cakepans, beginning at outer edge of pan.

Cover and repeat rising procedure 50 minutes or until doubled in bulk. Gently brush loaves with 1 egg and sprinkle with sesame seeds. Bake at 350° for 30 minutes or until golden brown. Cool loaves 10 minutes on wire racks before removing from pans. Yield: three 8-inch loaves.

Members of the Sons of Pericles present a Texas Centennial tableau, 1936.

VASILOPETA

¾ cup butter or margarine,
  softened
1½ cups sugar
6 cups all-purpose flour,
  divided
1½ cups milk, divided
3 eggs
1 tablespoon ground
  cinnamon
2 teaspoons baking
  powder
1 teaspoon baking soda
2 tablespoons grated
  orange rind
¼ cup orange juice
Whole cloves
Sesame seeds
1 (8-ounce) package
  blanched whole almonds
1 egg
1 teaspoon milk

Cream butter in a large mixing bowl; gradually add sugar, beating well. Add 4 cups flour alternately with 1 cup milk, beginning and ending with flour. Add 3 eggs and cinnamon, beating well.

Dissolve baking powder and soda in remaining ½ cup milk; add to creamed mixture, mixing well. Stir in orange rind, juice, and remaining 2 cups flour, mixing well.

Pour batter into a well-greased 10-inch springform pan. Outline the date of the New Year on top of cake using whole cloves and pushing stems into batter. Generously sprinkle entire surface of cake with sesame seeds. Outline cloves with whole almonds. Place remaining almonds around outside edge of cake top.

Combine egg and 1 teaspoon milk; beat well. Brush top of cake with egg mixture. Bake at 250° for 2½ hours or until a wooden pick inserted in center comes out clean. Cool in pan 20 minutes. Remove sides of pan. Cool completely before slicing. Yield: one 10-inch cake.

A montage of items picturing the mighty honey bee and his sweet gift to the world.

DIPLES

¼ teaspoon dry yeast
1½ tablespoons warm orange
  juice (105° to 115°)
3 eggs, beaten
3 tablespoons whiskey
Pinch of salt
2 cups all-purpose flour,
  divided
1½ cups water
1 cup sugar
½ cup honey
Vegetable oil
2 teaspoons ground
  cinnamon

Dissolve yeast in orange juice in a medium bowl; let stand 5 minutes. Add eggs, whiskey, salt, and 1 cup flour; beat at medium speed of an electric mixer until smooth. Add remaining flour; stir until well blended.

Shape dough into 1-inch balls. Place balls in a well-greased bowl, turning to grease top. Cover and let rise in a warm place (85°), free from drafts, 1 hour. (Balls will not double in bulk.)

Combine water and sugar in a small saucepan; bring to a boil. Reduce heat, and simmer 15 minutes. Stir in honey; bring to a boil, and immediately remove from heat. Set aside.

Roll each ball to ⅛-inch thickness; cut a 6- x 2-inch rectangle from each ball.

Drop strips, one at a time, into deep hot oil (375°). Using two forks, immediately roll each strip, jellyroll fashion. Cook until golden brown, turning once. Drain well on paper towels. Drizzle each rolled pastry with reserved syrup, and sprinkle with cinnamon. Yield: about 2 dozen.

SPECIAL DAYS

There are special days in the life of each of us which demand that some note be taken. They range from the simplest birthday party for a little child, to whom the candles on the cake are incredibly wondrous, to the reception held for an anniversary couple to whom the mere fact that someone remembered is happiness enough.

Some birthdays are especially remarkable. We're only sixteen once, or twenty-one. But these milestones seem quite different now from the same ages a century ago. Not many young people were still students at that age; many were married, possibly parents. High school and college have delayed what used to be looked upon as the age of maturation. At twenty-one, today's youth is frequently pushing to complete an undergraduate degree; male and female alike are heading into careers that did not exist in our grandparents' day. Consequently, people tend to marry later.

Actually, we are any age only once, and Southern families have always made much of birthdays; we don't wait until the century mark is reached to stage a birthday party.

Housewarmings are a long-standing tradition, but in older days, it was the people who moved or renovated a home who gave their own housewarming party, preparing the food for their friends. Now there is more likely to be a crowd of friends arriving at the new digs bearing food and drink ready for serving—right down to paper plates and cups, just in case the dishes haven't been unpacked. We have a menu in this chapter especially earmarked for toting to a housewarming. It is a landmark occurrence, whether the new occupants have just bought their first home or have simply rented a new apartment.

There is one time-honored tradition of which one hears little nowadays: the mortgage-burning celebration. It is seldom in our mobile society that a family settles in, once and for all, with the intention of actually paying off the omnipresent mortgage. Still, it does happen. And when it does, there stands the homestead free and clear, and it is worth celebrating. It is a perfect excuse to "make a ball." If one could find a house and a couple united for long enough to weather housewarming, anniversaries, and mortgage burning, now there would be a party to end all parties!

MENU OF MENUS

LITTLE FOLKS' BIRTHDAY

SWEET SIXTEEN

CELEBRATING
TWENTY-ONE

MOTHER'S DAY BRUNCH

ANNIVERSARY
CELEBRATION

A HOUSEWARMING
POTLUCK DINNER

"BURN THE MORTGAGE"
OPEN HOUSE

TEXAS BIRTHDAY DINNER

FATHER'S DAY ICE CREAM
PARTY

LITTLE FOLKS' BIRTHDAY

When a child is due a birthday celebration, some mothers have an innate genius for stage-managing such an affair. Others are on shaky ground: "I can't bake a fancy cake" is often heard. Here, for the timorous, is an easy cake baked to resemble an old-fashioned train. Invitations may take the form of a folded train ticket with time and place of departure (address) and return (party's over). Make a segment to tear off for the "ride," a game of musical chairs played with chairs lined up passenger-style. Another bit of ticket admits one to the "dining car" for ice cream and cake. Just remember: children are wonderfully uncritical. They'll love it.

CHOO-CHOO CHOCOLATE CAKE
ASSORTED ICE CREAMS
PINEAPPLE ORANGEADE

Serves 16 to 20

Choo-Choo Chocolate Cake sets the theme for a child's birthday party.

CHOO-CHOO CHOCOLATE CAKE

⅔ cup shortening, softened
1½ cups sugar
3 eggs
2 cups sifted cake flour
½ cup cocoa
1½ teaspoons baking powder
½ teaspoon baking soda
1 teaspoon salt
1 cup buttermilk
1 teaspoon vanilla extract
Chocolate Frosting
Decorator Icing
Yellow food coloring
7 peppermint rounds
6 vanilla wafers
Red licorice whips
1 sugar cone
Candy dots, assorted colors

Cream shortening; gradually add sugar, beating well. Add eggs, one at a time, beating well after each addition.

Combine flour, cocoa, baking powder, soda, and salt; add to creamed mixture alternately with buttermilk, beginning and ending with flour mixture. Stir in vanilla.

Pour batter into a greased and floured 13- x 9- x 2-inch baking pan. Bake at 350° for 35 minutes or until a wooden pick inserted in center comes out clean. Cool in pan 10 minutes; remove cake from pan, and cool completely on a wire rack. Freeze cake about 2 hours. (Cake will have clean edges when cut for assembly into train engine.)

Cut cake into two 10- x 4¼-inch rectangles; cut remaining cake into two 4¼- x 2½-inch rectangles. Spread Chocolate Frosting over top of one 10- x 4¼-inch rectangle. Top with remaining 10- x 4¼-inch rectangle; frost top, and set aside.

Align edges of two remaining 4¼- x 2½-inch rectangles to form a 5- x 4¼-inch rectangle. Spread Chocolate Frosting on cut edges of center seam to attach. Using a large metal spatula, carefully lift rectangle and place on top and at one end of larger frosted rectangle, aligning the 4½-inch edges. (One end of cake should have 3 layers arranged to resemble an engineer's station at rear of train engine.) Trim sides of cake to make layers even, and remove any excess cake crumbs, if necessary. Spread remaining Chocolate Frosting over top and on all sides of cake.

Place about 2 cups Decorator Icing in a small mixing bowl. Add yellow food coloring to reach desired tint, mixing well. Reserve remaining icing for additional colors, if desired.

Fill a pastry bag with yellow Decorator Icing; pipe icing attractively onto edges of frosted cake and outline details (such as windows) to resemble a train "engine."

Using Decorator Icing, attach 6 peppermint rounds to 6 vanilla wafers for wheels. Connect wheels with licorice whips; secure to engine with Decorator Icing. Cut away lower portion of the sugar cone; discard larger end. Decorate cone with icing, and insert at front of engine to resemble smoke stack. Place a peppermint round in center of front of engine. Pipe icing attractively around peppermints and engine wheels. Use candy dots to decorate cake as desired. Serve cake with ice cream. Yield: 16 to 20 servings.

Chocolate Frosting:

¾ cup butter or margarine, softened
5¼ cups sifted powdered sugar
¼ cup cocoa
½ cup plus 2 tablespoons whipping cream
1½ teaspoons vanilla extract

Cream butter. Combine sugar and cocoa; gradually add to butter alternately with whipping cream, beating well. Add vanilla; beat until mixture is smooth. Yield: frosting for one 13- x 9-inch cake.

Decorator Icing:

1 (16-ounce) package plus 2 cups sifted powdered sugar
1 cup shortening
⅓ cup water
¼ teaspoon salt
1 teaspoon vanilla extract

Combine sugar and shortening in a medium mixing bowl; beat at low speed of an electric mixer until smooth. Add water slowly; beat 10 minutes. Add salt and vanilla; mix well.

Decorator Icing will keep in an airtight container in refrigerator for up to 1 week. Yield: about 3 cups.

Outdoor birthday party at Brook Hill Estate, Richmond, Virginia, c.1910.

PINEAPPLE ORANGEADE

4 (20-ounce) cans sliced
  pineapple in heavy syrup,
  undrained
6 cups fresh orange juice
2 cup cold water
Crushed ice

    Drain pineapple, reserving syrup; set 3 pineapple slices aside for garnish. Reserve remaining pineapple slices for other uses.
    Combine pineapple syrup, orange juice, and water in a large serving pitcher; mix well. Add reserved pineapple slices for garnish. Serve over crushed ice. Yield: 16 to 20 servings.

President Benjamin Harrison's tenancy in the White House (1889-1893) was, to some minds, somewhat forgettable. His was not a notably colorful personality, but the Harrisons entertained properly, if not spectacularly. By all accounts, he was a different person when playing with his children and grandchildren. An especially endearing story is told of a grandchild's birthday, when fifteen highchairs were lined up at the dining table. The fern centerpiece had two flags crossed over it, and the refreshments were splendid. The president delighted each and every small guest by dancing with them one by one.

SWEET SIXTEEN

Sweet sixteen! It is a magical time for the maturing Southern girl, definitely a party day. How different her lot from that of her Colonial forebears, when girls of wealthy families were taught the rudiments of a liberal arts education but were emphatically trained in the "housewifely arts."

Sweet sixteen might have been, and frequently was, already a wife and mother. Her sphere was usually small and mundane. Our sixteen is a different matter; on her way to becoming her own person, all she needs is a crowd of friends, a neat party, and the keys to a car, preferably her own.

  HERO SANDWICHES
POTATO CHIPS * ICED SOFT DRINKS
SWEET SIXTEEN BIRTHDAY CAKE

Serves 10 to 12

HERO SANDWICHES

2 (16-ounce) loaves Italian bread
½ cup mayonnaise
¼ cup plus 2 tablespoons Dijon mustard
Leaf lettuce
2 medium tomatoes, sliced
1 (8-ounce) package sliced corned beef
1 (8-ounce) package sliced salami
1 (8-ounce) package sliced bologna
1 (4-ounce) package sliced breast of turkey
1 (8-ounce) package Swiss cheese slices
1 (8-ounce) package mild Cheddar cheese slices
1 (6-ounce) package provolone cheese slices

Using an electric knife or sharp bread knife, slice each loaf in half lengthwise.

Spread cut side of top of each loaf with ¼ cup mayonnaise; spread cut side of bottom of each loaf with 3 tablespoons mustard. Line bottom of each loaf with leaf lettuce; top lettuce with half of tomato slices.

Arrange meat slices and cheese slices evenly over tomatoes on each loaf, alternating meat and cheese. Top each with remaining tomato slices, and cover with tops of bread loaves. Slice sandwiches and serve. Yield: 10 to 12 servings.

Early 1900s postcard for a sixteenth birthday.

Hero Sandwiches, chips, soft drinks, and a cake say "Happy Sweet Sixteenth!"

SWEET SIXTEEN BIRTHDAY CAKE

1 cup butter or margarine, softened
2 cups sugar
1 egg
5 egg yolks
3 cups all-purpose flour
2½ teaspoons baking powder
1¾ cups milk
2 teaspoons vanilla extract
Fluffy Butter Frosting
Yellow food coloring

Cream butter in a large mixing bowl; gradually add sugar, beating well. Add egg and yolks, mixing well.

Combine flour and baking powder, stirring well. Gradually add to creamed mixture alternately with milk, beginning and ending with flour mixture. Stir in vanilla.

Pour batter into a greased and floured 13- x 9- x 2-inch baking pan. Bake at 325° for 55 minutes or until cake tests done.

Cool cake in pan 10 minutes; invert onto cake platter, and cool completely.

Place two-thirds of Fluffy Butter Frosting in a large mixing bowl; add yellow food coloring to tint to desired shade. Mix well. Frost top and sides of cake. Place remaining Fluffy Butter Frosting in pastry bag; attractively pipe frosting onto top and around edges of cake. Yield: one 13- x 9-inch cake.

Fluffy Butter Frosting:

¼ cup plus 2 tablespoons butter, softened
¼ teaspoon salt
1 teaspoon vanilla extract
4 cups sifted powdered sugar
2 egg whites

Combine butter, salt, and vanilla in a large mixing bowl; beat until well blended. Gradually add sugar alternately with egg whites; beat well. Yield: frosting for one 13- x 9-inch cake.

O ur Colonials took a girl's competence in music and dancing for granted. But Tidewater aristocrats such as William Byrd of Westover expected more of their own. Byrd once bragged to an Englishman that his daughters were daily "up to their elbows in housewifery, which will qualify them effectually for useful wives and, if they live long enough, for notable women."

CELEBRATING TWENTY-ONE

On November 12, 1890, Allan Talbott, a member of a prominent Virginia family, was accorded a twenty-first birthday feast, the importance of which is amply illustrated by the fact that the menu reposes in the archives of the Virginia Historical Society. Mr. Talbott had attained his majority, and by tradition, that birthday is a kind of watershed. Childish things are put aside; manhood and womanhood come with their duties. We have not lost the significance of the twenty-first. Here we put away the soft drinks and hero sandwiches of sweet sixteen and pop the champagne to accompany such grown-up viands as oysters and beef tenderloin.

OYSTERS ON THE HALF SHELL
or
INDIVIDUAL LIVER PÂTÉ ON TOAST ROUNDS
SHERRIED CONSOMMÉ
ROAST TENDERLOIN OF BEEF WITH MUSHROOMS
TOMATOES STUFFED WITH SPINACH ROCKEFELLER
FRESH FRUIT WITH ROQUEFORT CHEESE
CHAMPAGNE

Serves 12

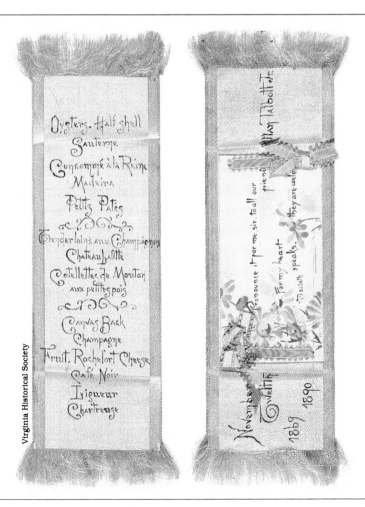

Virginia Historical Society

For Allan Talbott, Jr.'s twenty-first birthday party, the invitation and menu were lettered on gold ribbon.

Mr. Talbott's party was not extravagant by pre-Revolutionary War standards. In Williamsburg, the birthday of the reigning monarch was the social event of the season. Fireworks and salutes of cannon went on all day. The evening was given over to a "Grand Entertainment": Dancing went on all night. And drinking . . . not, it was hoped, enough to cause disorder or disaster. Wealthy planters, when the monarchy was no more, took to celebrating their own birthdays in a manner fit for royalty. Mr. Talbott's party was part and parcel of an ongoing heritage to which he had been born.

INDIVIDUAL LIVER PÂTÉ ON TOAST ROUNDS

½ cup plus 2 tablespoons
  butter or margarine, divided
½ cup finely chopped onion
¼ pound chicken livers
¼ pound fresh mushrooms,
  sliced
1½ teaspoons seasoned salt
Dash of pepper
Dash of red pepper
1 teaspoon lemon juice
2 hard-cooked eggs, quartered
1 (2¼-ounce) package
  pistachio nuts, chopped

Melt ½ cup butter in a large skillet; add onion, and sauté until golden brown. Add chicken livers and mushrooms. Cook, stirring frequently, 5 minutes or until livers are tender. Add remaining butter, seasoned salt, pepper, and lemon juice; stir until butter melts. Cool.

Divide mixture into 4 equal portions. Combine 1 portion of liver mixture with 2 egg quarters in container of an electric blender; process until very smooth. Transfer to a mixing bowl. Repeat procedure with remaining portions of mixture, blending each portion separately. Stir nuts into liver mixture, and mix well.

Press pâté in miniature molds. Cover and chill 8 hours or overnight; unmold. Serve on melba toast rounds. Yield: about 2 dozen.

SHERRIED CONSOMMÉ

8 (10½-ounce) cans beef
  consommé
½ teaspoon pepper
1 cup sherry
½ cup chopped green onion
  tops

Place consommé and pepper in a large Dutch oven; bring to a boil. Remove from heat; add sherry, and stir well. Garnish each serving with green onion tops. Serve hot. Yield: 12 cups.

1911 postcard: A modest but welcome invitation to a party.

ROAST TENDERLOIN OF BEEF WITH MUSHROOMS

1 (4- to 4½-pound) beef
  tenderloin, trimmed
1 teaspoon salt
½ teaspoon pepper
½ teaspoon garlic powder
½ cup Burgundy, or other dry
  red wine
½ cup water
4 cups sliced fresh
  mushrooms
2 tablespoons chopped fresh
  parsley

Rub tenderloin with salt, pepper, and garlic powder. Place tenderloin on a rack in a shallow roasting pan. Tuck narrow end under to make roast more uniformly thick. Insert meat thermometer, if desired.

Bake, uncovered, at 450° for 45 minutes or until meat thermometer registers 140° (rare). Cover; set aside and keep warm.

Combine wine, water, mushrooms, and parsley in a medium saucepan. Bring to a boil; reduce heat, and simmer 10 minutes or until mushrooms are tender.

Cut tenderloin into 1-inch-thick slices, and arrange on a heated platter. Serve with mushroom sauce. Yield: 12 servings.

TOMATOES STUFFED WITH SPINACH ROCKEFELLER

4 (10-ounce) packages frozen
  chopped spinach
12 large firm tomatoes
1 cup finely chopped onion
½ cup butter or margarine
1 cup seasoned fine dry
  breadcrumbs
4 eggs, beaten
2 teaspoons salt
1 teaspoon dried whole thyme
¼ cup plus 2 tablespoons
  grated Parmesan cheese

Cook spinach according to package directions. Drain and set aside.

Remove stems from tomatoes, and cut a ¼-inch slice from the top of each. Scoop out pulp, leaving shells intact. Reserve pulp for use in another recipe. Invert tomato shells on paper towels to drain; set aside.

Sauté onion in butter in a medium saucepan over low heat until tender. Add spinach, breadcrumbs, eggs, salt, and thyme; stir well. Spoon mixture into prepared tomato shells. Sprinkle cheese over top of tomatoes. Place tomatoes in two lightly greased baking dishes. Bake at 350° for 20 minutes or until browned. Serve immediately. Yield: 12 servings.

Individual Liver Pâté on Toast Rounds, with Champagne. Cheers!

73

TEXAS BIRTHDAY DINNER

Here is a hearty birthday dinner that goes back a few generations to the days when city was city and country was country. This menu was put together in honor of the patriarch of a Texas farm family in 1927, when some three generations of good cooks each prepared her best dish, from fried chicken to angel food cake. Their ice cream was handcranked; today the farm kitchen's deep freeze is packed with time-saving comestibles, like commercial ice cream. Most of the distinctions between town and country have faded, not only in foodways but in education, travel, and other sophistications. Down South, rural or urbane, we still go all out for birthdays.

TEXAS FRIED CHICKEN
FRIED HAM WITH CREAM GRAVY
BAKED BEANS
SQUASH CASSEROLE
PERFECTION SALAD * FRESH FRUIT SALAD
CORN STICKS
BIRTHDAY LAYER CAKE
or
ANGEL FOOD CAKE WITH ICE CREAM BALLS

Serves 12 to 15

Houston Metropolitan Research Center, Houston Public Library

A 1911 postcard brings birthday wishes.

TEXAS FRIED CHICKEN

3 (3½- to 4-pound)
   broiler-fryers, cut up
3 tablespoons salt
1 tablespoon pepper
3 (5.33-ounce) cans
   evaporated milk
All-purpose flour
3 cups shortening
Fresh parsley sprigs (optional)

Sprinkle surface of chicken with salt and pepper. Place chicken in a shallow pan, and pour milk over top. Cover and refrigerate 1 hour. Remove chicken from milk, and dredge in flour. Discard milk.

Heat shortening in a large skillet to 325°; fill with chicken pieces and fry, uncovered, 5 minutes or until brown. Reduce heat; cover and cook an additional 30 minutes or until chicken is tender. Drain chicken well on paper towels. Repeat procedure with remaining chicken pieces.

Place chicken on a warm serving platter, and garnish with parsley sprigs, if desired. Yield: 12 to 15 servings.

*A gathering of family
and friends share in
a spread of their own
making near Galveston,
Texas, February, 1911.*

FRIED HAM WITH CREAM GRAVY

6 to 8 (¼-inch-thick)
   center-cut smoked ham
   slices
¼ cup all-purpose flour
2 cups milk

Trim fat from ham slices, leaving ¼-inch fat around edges. Score fat at 1-inch intervals to prevent slices from curling.

Heat a large skillet over low heat. Place first ham slice in skillet, fat side of ham near edge of skillet. Place second slice on top of first, with fat side of ham near opposite edge of skillet. Stack remaining ham slices, overlapping each slice so that fat side is near edge of skillet. Cover and cook over low heat 10 minutes. Remove ham from skillet. Turn over each slice, and return slices to skillet, repeating stacking procedure. Cover and continue cooking an additional 10 minutes. Transfer ham slices to a warm serving platter, and set aside.

Drain pan drippings, reserving ¼ cup in skillet. Add flour to drippings, stirring until smooth. Cook over low heat 1 minute, stirring constantly. Gradually add milk; cook over medium heat, stirring constantly, until thickened and bubbly. Serve gravy with ham. Yield: 12 to 15 servings.

BAKED BEANS

1 (16-ounce) package dried
   navy beans
½ pound salt pork
½ cup molasses
½ cup catsup
3 tablespoons sugar
1 tablespoon Worcestershire
   sauce
1 tablespoon dry mustard
1½ teaspoons salt
¼ teaspoon pepper
1 small onion, chopped

Sort and wash beans; place in a large bowl. Cover with water 2 inches above beans; cover and refrigerate overnight. Drain.

Place beans and salt pork in a large Dutch oven; cover with water 2 inches above beans. Bring to a boil. Cover; reduce heat, and simmer 30 minutes. Drain, reserving 2 cups liquid. Cut pork into 3 slices, and set aside.

Combine molasses, catsup, sugar, Worcestershire sauce, mustard, salt, pepper, and onion; stir well. Stir in beans, salt pork, and reserved liquid. Pour mixture into a 3-quart casserole. Cover and bake at 250° for 6 hours. Uncover and bake 1 additional hour. Yield: 12 to 15 servings.

SQUASH CASSEROLE

2 pounds yellow squash, sliced
1 medium onion, chopped
1 cup finely chopped celery
¼ cup finely chopped green pepper
¼ cup butter or margarine
1 cup (4 ounces) shredded sharp Cheddar cheese
⅔ cup coarsely crumbled crackers
4 eggs, beaten
2½ cups milk
1 teaspoon salt
¼ teaspoon pepper

Place squash and water to cover in a medium saucepan. Bring to a boil. Reduce heat; cover and cook 10 minutes. Drain well. Mash squash; drain once again. Set aside.

Sauté onion, celery, and green pepper in butter in a large skillet until vegetables are tender; remove from heat. Stir in squash, cheese, cracker crumbs, eggs, milk, salt, and pepper.

Pour mixture into a 12- x 8- x 2-inch baking dish. Bake, uncovered, at 375° for 30 minutes. Serve immediately. Yield: 12 to 15 servings.

PERFECTION SALAD

2 envelopes unflavored gelatin
½ cup water
2 (14½-ounce) cans whole tomatoes, chopped and undrained
½ cup vinegar
2 tablespoons sugar
1 tablespoon lemon juice
1 teaspoon salt
2 bay leaves
1 cup chopped cabbage
3 tablespoons finely chopped onion
3 tablespoons chopped pimiento
Lettuce leaves
Chopped cabbage
Mayonnaise
Paprika (optional)

Soften gelatin in water; set aside. Combine tomatoes, vinegar, sugar, lemon juice, salt, and bay leaves in a medium saucepan; bring to a boil. Remove from heat, and add softened gelatin, stirring until gelatin dissolves. Cool. Chill mixture until the consistency of unbeaten egg whites.

Remove and discard bay leaves. Fold in cabbage, onion, and pimiento; pour mixture into a lightly oiled 5-cup mold. Chill until firm.

Unmold salad onto a chilled, lettuce-lined plate. Sprinkle chopped cabbage around salad. Place a dollop of mayonnaise on top of salad, and sprinkle with paprika, if desired. Serve immediately. Yield: 12 to 15 servings.

FRESH FRUIT SALAD

9 oranges, peeled, seeded, and sectioned
1 large fresh pineapple, peeled, cored, and cut into spears
3 large bananas, peeled and cut into ½-inch slices
¾ pound red grapes, halved and seeded
¾ cup maraschino cherries
1 cup sugar
Lettuce leaves

Layer oranges, pineapple, bananas, grapes, and cherries in a large colander; sprinkle with sugar. Place colander over a large mixing bowl. Refrigerate. Let fruit juices drain into mixing bowl until ready to serve.

To serve, toss fruit and place in a lettuce-lined bowl; pour juices over fruit. Yield: 12 to 15 servings.

CORN STICKS

3 cups white cornmeal
1 cup all-purpose flour
¼ cup sugar
1 teaspoon salt
1 teaspoon baking powder
2 cups buttermilk
4 eggs, beaten
¼ cup shortening, melted

Combine first 5 ingredients; mix well. Add buttermilk and eggs, stirring just until dry ingredients are moistened. Stir shortening into batter.

Heat well-greased cast-iron corn stick pans in a 400° oven for 3 minutes or until very hot. Remove from oven; spoon batter into pans, filling three-fourths full. Bake at 400° for 25 minutes or until lightly browned. Yield: 2 dozen.

Wealthy plantation owners patterned their birthday observances after those of royalty. The birthday of Arthur Middleton is still celebrated in June at Middleton Place, near Charleston. Arthur's father, Henry, built the famous gardens at Middleton Place and was a delegate to the first Continental Congress in 1774; Arthur was a signer of the Declaration of Independence. His birthday is celebrated with musket fire and such lawn games as hoop rolling and sack races. People come from all around for the pageantry, the fife and drums, and, at sundown, a concert of eighteenth-century music.

Top off a birthday dinner with a real-life, homemade Angel Food Cake and Neopolitan Ice Cream Balls.

BIRTHDAY LAYER CAKE

1 cup butter or margarine, softened
1¾ cups sugar
6 eggs
2 cups all-purpose flour
1 teaspoon baking powder
¼ cup milk
2 teaspoons almond extract
Butter Frosting
Candied fruit slices
Gumdrops
Birthday candles

Cream butter in a large mixing bowl; gradually add sugar, beating until light and fluffy. Add eggs, one at a time, beating well after each addition.

Combine flour and baking powder; stir well. Add to creamed mixture alternately with milk, beginning and ending with flour mixture. Stir in almond extract.

Pour batter into two 9-inch round cakepans. Bake at 350° for 25 minutes or until a wooden pick inserted in center comes out clean. Cool in pans 10 minutes; remove layers from pans, and let cool completely on wire racks.

Spread Butter Frosting between layers and on top and sides of cake. Place candied fruit around sides of cake. Using gumdrops as holders for birthday candles, arrange on top of cake. Yield: one 2-layer cake.

Butter Frosting:

2 egg whites
¼ cup butter, softened
1 teaspoon almond extract
3 cups sifted powdered sugar

Beat egg whites (at room temperature) in a medium mixing bowl until foamy. Add softened butter, beating until well blended. Add almond extract; beat well. Gradually add powdered sugar, beating until well blended. Yield: frosting for one 2-layer cake.

ANGEL FOOD CAKE WITH ICE CREAM BALLS

10 egg whites
1 teaspoon cream of tartar
¼ teaspoon salt
½ teaspoon vanilla extract
½ teaspoon almond extract
1¼ cups sugar
1 cup sifted cake flour
Neopolitan ice cream balls

Beat egg whites (at room temperature) until foamy. Add cream of tartar and salt; beat until soft peaks form. Add flavorings; beat well. Gradually add sugar, 2 tablespoons at a time, beating until stiff peaks form. Sprinkle flour over egg white mixture, ¼ cup at a time, folding in carefully.

Spoon batter into an ungreased 10-inch tube pan, spreading evenly with a spatula. Bake at 325° for 45 minutes or until cake springs back when lightly touched. Remove from oven, and invert pan. Cool 40 minutes; remove cake to a large serving platter. Arrange ice cream balls around cake, and serve immediately. Yield: one 10-inch cake.

MOTHER'S DAY BRUNCH

Anna M. Jarvis (1864-1948) began the custom of celebrating Mother's Day on May 10, 1908, when she requested her minister in Grafton, West Virginia, to hold a special service. On the same day, a similar service was held in Philadelphia, where her mother had died. Many people today honor their mothers by wearing a carnation to church on Mother's Day, the second Sunday in May. And what mother would not enjoy this brunch, filled with subtle flavors and colorful as a rainbow?

FRESH ORANGE JUICE
or
PEACH DAIQUIRI
CANADIAN BACON SPECIAL
EGGS WITH BRANDIED CREAM SAUCE
FRESH STRAWBERRIES AND BLUEBERRIES
GEORGIA PECAN MUFFINS

Serves 4

PEACH DAIQUIRI

1 (10-ounce) package frozen peaches, thawed
1 (6-ounce) can frozen pink lemonade concentrate, thawed and undiluted
¾ cup light rum
Cracked ice

Combine half each of peaches, lemonade, and rum in container of an electric blender; process until smooth. Gradually add cracked ice, processing until mixture reaches desired consistency. Pour into serving glasses.

Repeat procedure with remaining ingredients. Yield: about 5 cups.

CANADIAN BACON SPECIAL

8 (¼-inch-thick) slices Canadian bacon
½ cup cola-flavored carbonated beverage

Place bacon and cola in a heavy skillet; cover and cook over medium heat 15 minutes, turning once. Place bacon on a serving platter, and spoon any remaining cola over slices. Yield: 4 servings.

West Virginia Department of Culture and History

Anna Jarvis founded Mother's Day to honor her mother.

EGGS WITH BRANDIED CREAM SAUCE

2 cups seasoned croutons
2 tablespoons butter or
  margarine, melted
4 poached eggs
1 cup (4 ounces) shredded
  sharp Cheddar cheese
Brandied Cream Sauce
Paprika
Fresh parsley sprigs

Combine croutons and butter, tossing well. Place on a serving plate. Arrange eggs over croutons. Sprinkle each egg with ¼ cup cheese. Spoon Brandied Cream Sauce over eggs; sprinkle with paprika. Garnish with parsley sprigs. Serve immediately. Yield: 4 servings.

Brandied Cream Sauce:

2 tablespoons butter or
  margarine
2 tablespoons all-purpose
  flour
¾ cup evaporated milk
¼ cup chicken broth
2 tablespoons brandy
¼ teaspoon salt

Melt butter in a saucepan over low heat; add flour, stirring until smooth. Cook 1 minute, stirring constantly. Gradually add milk and broth; cook over medium heat, stirring constantly, until mixture is thickened and bubbly. Stir in brandy and salt. Yield: 1 cup.

While Mother's Day is a relatively new holiday in America, its origins go back to seventeenth-century England, when indentured young persons were allowed to visit their mothers once a year. "Mothering Sunday" saw them heading for home, carrying a gift, perhaps a simnel or "mothering" cake. Mother was queen for a day; the family attended church, and then dinner was prepared in her honor.

GEORGIA PECAN MUFFINS

2 cups all-purpose flour
3 tablespoons sugar
1 tablespoon plus 1 teaspoon
  baking powder
½ teaspoon salt
2 eggs, beaten
1 cup milk
¼ cup butter or margarine,
  melted
½ cup finely chopped pecans

Combine flour, sugar, baking powder, and salt; make a well in center of mixture. Add eggs and milk; stir just until dry ingredients are moistened. Add butter and pecans; stir just until blended.

Spoon batter into greased muffin tins, filling three-fourths full. Bake at 425° for 20 minutes or until lightly browned. Yield: 1 dozen.

FATHER'S DAY ICE CREAM PARTY

There were several unconnected beginnings for Father's Day. The first observance, while it did not catch fire as a national movement, was held in West Virginia in 1908. Mrs. John Bruce Dodd was influential in getting a city-wide observance held in Spokane, Washington, in 1910. But Harry C. Meek of Chicago gets credit for en-larging the scope of Father's Day so it could go national. In 1915, he began pushing the idea during speeches to various Lion's clubs that established the third Sunday in June for honoring fathers; it was, by coincidence, the same date fixed in Spokane earlier. Homemade ice cream is made to order for this day, along with the good toppings.

VANILLA ICE CREAM
CARAMEL ICE CREAM
BANANA-FRUIT ICE CREAM
PEANUT BUTTER SAUCE
CHOCOLATE SAUCE
CHOPPED NUTS * SLICED FRUIT
ICEBOX COOKIES

Serves 12

Irene Dunne and William Powell starred in Life With Father, *1947.*

VANILLA ICE CREAM

2¼ cups sugar
¼ cup plus 2 tablespoons
   all-purpose flour
½ teaspoon salt
5 cups milk, scalded
6 eggs, beaten
1 quart whipping cream
1½ tablespoons vanilla
   extract

Combine sugar, flour, and salt in a 3-quart saucepan; gradually stir in milk. Cook over medium heat 15 minutes or until thickened, stirring constantly.

Stir one-fourth of hot mixture into beaten eggs; add to remaining hot mixture, stirring constantly. Cook 1 minute; remove from heat, and cool to room temperature. Chill 2 hours.

Combine whipping cream and vanilla in a large bowl; add chilled custard, stirring with a wire whisk to combine. Pour mixture into freezer can of a 1-gallon hand-turned or electric freezer. Freeze according to manufacturer's instructions. Let ripen 1½ to 2 hours before serving. Yield: 1 gallon.

With three ice cream recipes, two sauces, nuts, and fruit, plus Icebox Cookies, the imagination reaches new heights.

When *Life With Father* was released in 1947, it was a pre-ordained success. Based on the hit Broadway play by Howard Lindsay and Russel Crouse (from a *New Yorker* story by Clarence Day), it was "star-studded." Along with Dunne and Powell were Edmund Gwenn and Zasu Pitts, and such newcomers as Elizabeth Taylor, Jimmy Lydon, and Martin Milner. "Say 'Sayzoo!' " insisted Zasu, whose popularity endured from silent films to television. Among friends Zasu was known for her fine cooking: Her book, *Candy Hits*, came out in 1963.

CARAMEL ICE CREAM

½ cup cornstarch
¼ cup milk
6 cups milk, scalded
3 cups sugar, divided
4 eggs, beaten
2 cups half-and-half
1 tablespoon vanilla extract

Combine cornstarch and ¼ cup milk; stir until smooth. Combine scalded milk, 2 cups sugar, eggs, and cornstarch mixture in a large Dutch oven; stir until well blended, and set aside.

Sprinkle remaining sugar evenly in a 10-inch cast-iron skillet; place over medium heat. Caramelize sugar by constantly stirring with a wooden spoon. Remove sugar from heat, and gradually pour into milk mixture in Dutch oven.

Cook over medium heat, stirring constantly, until smooth and thickened. Remove from heat; cool. Stir in half-and-half and vanilla.

Pour into freezer can of a 1-gallon hand-turned or electric freezer. Freeze according to manufacturer's instructions. Let ripen at least 1 hour before serving. Yield: about 1 gallon.

BANANA-FRUIT ICE CREAM

1 (16-ounce) can apricot
  halves, undrained
1 large banana, sliced
¾ cup fresh orange juice
1 cup sugar
1 quart milk
2 cups whipping cream
1 (14-ounce) can sweetened
  condensed milk
¼ teaspoon salt

Drain apricots, reserving liquid. Set liquid aside.

Place apricots and banana slices in container of an electric blender; process on high speed 10 seconds or until pureed.

Combine pureed mixture, reserved apricot liquid, orange juice, and sugar in a large mixing bowl; stir well. Chill thoroughly before continuing.

Stir milk, whipping cream, condensed milk, and salt into chilled fruit mixture. Pour into freezer can of a 1-gallon hand-turned or electric freezer. Freeze according to manufacturer's instructions. Let ripen 1 hour before serving. Yield: 1 gallon.

If this ad appeared today, it might mention potassium.

PEANUT BUTTER SAUCE

2 cups firmly packed light
  brown sugar
1 cup whipping cream
2 tablespoons butter or
  margarine
½ cup creamy peanut butter

Combine first 3 ingredients in a Dutch oven; cook over low heat, stirring frequently, 15 minutes or until sugar dissolves. Remove from heat, and add peanut butter; stir until smooth. Serve immediately over ice cream. Yield: about 2¼ cups.

CHOCOLATE SAUCE

1 cup butter or margarine
4 (1-ounce) squares
  unsweetened chocolate
1 (16-ounce) package
  powdered sugar, sifted
1 (13-ounce) can evaporated
  milk

Melt butter and chocolate in top of a double boiler; stir in powdered sugar and evaporated milk. Cook over medium heat, stirring until sauce is smooth. Serve warm over ice cream. Yield: 4½ cups.

ICEBOX COOKIES

1 cup butter or margarine,
  softened
1 cup firmly packed brown
  sugar
1 cup sugar
2 eggs
3½ cups self-rising flour
1 teaspoon vanilla extract
1 cup finely chopped pecans

Combine butter and sugar; beat well. Add eggs, flour, and vanilla; mix well. Stir in pecans.

Divide dough into three equal portions; shape each portion into a 12- x 2-inch roll. Wrap in waxed paper, and refrigerate overnight.

Slice dough into ¼-inch-thick slices; place slices on ungreased baking sheets. Bake at 350° for 10 minutes or until lightly browned. Remove to wire racks to cool. Yield: 9 dozen.

ANNIVERSARY CELEBRATION

Silver and Golden anniversaries are one-of-a-kind occurrences; celebration is in order. When a couple reach a point in their lives at which they can look back over that many years of sickness and health, they richly deserve to regard themselves as a rousing success story. Twenty-five . . . fifty . . . years; where did the time go? Often an open-house reception is given by children of the honorees. Other couples have been known to do the honors themselves, inviting their old friends, sometimes reuniting members of the original wedding party. It is a time for sharing memories and for cutting a shimmering silver or gold cake with a number on it.

SILVER ANNIVERSARY CAKE
or
LEMON GOLD CAKE
EGG SALAD FINGER SANDWICHES
MINT ROSES
SALTED PECANS
GOLDEN MINT PUNCH
or
FRUITED CHAMPAGNE PUNCH

Serves 24

SILVER ANNIVERSARY CAKE

1½ cups shortening
2¼ cups sugar
4½ cups sifted cake flour
1 tablespoon plus 1½
   teaspoons baking powder
½ teaspoon salt
1¾ cups milk
¾ teaspoon almond
   extract
9 egg whites
Divinity Frosting
Silver ribbon
Silver balls
Miniature bride and groom

Cream shortening; gradually add sugar, beating until light and fluffy. Combine flour, baking powder, and salt; add to creamed mixture alternately with milk, beginning and ending with flour mixture. Stir in almond extract.

Beat egg whites (at room temperature) until stiff peaks form; fold into batter. Spoon batter into 1 greased and floured 8-inch round cakepan and 1 greased and floured 10-inch round cakepan. Bake 8-inch layer at 350° for 30 minutes and 10-inch layer at 350° for 45 minutes or until a wooden pick inserted in center comes out clean. Cool in pans 10 minutes; remove layers from pans, and cool completely on wire racks.

Slice each layer in half horizontally; spread Divinity Frosting between sliced layers, placing larger layer, bottom side down, on cake plate. Spread top and sides of bottom layer with Divinity Frosting. Place smaller layer, bottom side down, in middle of larger layer. Spread top and sides of top layer with Divinity Frosting. Decorate with silver ribbon and balls, and place miniature bride and groom on top layer. Yield: one 10-inch tier cake.

Divinity Frosting:

3 cups sugar
1 cup water
Pinch of salt
6 egg whites

Combine sugar, water, and salt in a medium saucepan; cook over medium heat, stirring occasionally, until mixture reaches soft ball stage (240°).

Beat egg whites (at room temperature) in a large bowl until foamy. While beating at medium speed of an electric mixer, slowly pour syrup in a thin stream over egg whites. Turn mixer to high speed; beat until stiff peaks form and frosting is thick enough to spread. Frost cake immediately. Yield: enough frosting for one 2-layer cake.

LEMON GOLD CAKE

1 cup butter or margarine, softened
2 cups sugar
4 eggs
3 cups all-purpose flour
2 teaspoons cream of tartar
1 teaspoon baking soda
1 cup milk
½ teaspoon vanilla extract
½ teaspoon lemon extract
Lemon Butter Cream Frosting
Lemon rind bows (optional)

Cream butter in a large mixing bowl; gradually add sugar, beating well. Add eggs, one at a time, beating well after each addition.

Combine flour, cream of tartar, and soda; add to creamed mixture alternately with milk, beginning and ending with flour mixture. Stir in flavorings.

Pour batter into 3 greased and floured 9-inch round cakepans. Bake at 350° for 25 minutes or until a wooden pick inserted in center comes out clean. Cool in pans 10 minutes; remove layers from pans, and cool completely on wire racks.

Spread Lemon Butter Cream Frosting between layers and on top and sides of cake. Garnish top of cake with lemon rind bows, if desired. Yield: one 3-layer cake.

Lemon Butter Cream Frosting:

½ cup butter or margarine, softened
½ cup shortening
1 teaspoon vanilla extract
½ teaspoon lemon extract
2 teaspoons grated lemon rind
4 cups sifted powdered sugar
¼ cup plus 2 tablespoons milk
Yellow food coloring

Combine butter and shortening, beating until light and fluffy. Add flavorings and lemon rind, beating well. Add powdered sugar and milk alternately, beating until spreading consistency. Add yellow food coloring to desired tint; beat until smooth. Yield: frosting for one 3-layer cake.

EGG SALAD FINGER SANDWICHES

12 hard-cooked eggs, chopped
¼ cup butter or margarine, softened
2 tablespoons commercial French dressing
2 teaspoons Worcestershire sauce
½ teaspoon prepared mustard
Pinch of salt
48 slices white bread
24 slices wheat bread
Whipped butter

Combine eggs, ¼ cup butter, French dressing, Worcestershire sauce, mustard, and salt; stir until well blended. Chill.

Trim crust from bread; cut into 2-inch rounds. Lightly spread whipped butter on one slice of white bread and one slice of wheat bread; spread egg salad on each slice. Stack bread, placing wheat on top, and cover with a white bread round. Slice sandwich in half vertically. Repeat with remaining bread and egg mixture. Yield: 4 dozen.

A Golden Anniversary couple with friend, Dublin, Georgia. 1911 photograph.

MINT ROSES

1 (8-ounce) package cream cheese, softened
¼ teaspoon oil of peppermint
Yellow food coloring
6¾ to 9 cups sifted powdered sugar
Granulated sugar

Combine cream cheese and oil of peppermint; beat well. Divide mixture in half. Add yellow food coloring to half of mixture to reach desired color.

Add powdered sugar to both mixtures, kneading by hand until the consistency of a stiff dough. Shape mixture into ¾-inch balls; coat one side of ball with granulated sugar. Press balls into rose-shaped candy molds, sugar-coated side down. Unmold onto waxed paper immediately. Let dry 6 hours on each side. Yield: about 6 dozen.

Silver Cake and Golden Mint Punch are perfect for an anniversary celebration

Several generations pose for family photograph as Mr. and Mrs. Elmendorf celebrate their Golden Wedding Anniversary, San Antonio, 1900.

Daughters of the Republic of Texas Library at the Alamo, San Antonio, Texas

SALTED PECANS

¾ cup butter
6 cups pecan halves
1½ tablespoons salt

Place butter in a 13- x 9- x 2-inch baking pan; place in a 350° oven for 10 minutes or until butter melts.

Remove from oven; add pecans, and sprinkle with salt. Bake at 350° for 15 minutes, stirring after 10 minutes. Drain on paper towels. Yield: 6 cups.

GOLDEN MINT PUNCH

3 cups fresh mint sprigs
2 cups sugar
2 quarts water
1 (46-ounce) can pineapple juice, chilled
1 cup thinly sliced lemon rind
2 cups lemon juice, chilled
1 (33.8-ounce) bottle ginger ale, chilled
1 (28-ounce) bottle tonic water, chilled
Additional mint sprigs

Combine 3 cups mint sprigs, sugar, and water in a large Dutch oven, stirring well. Bring to a boil. Reduce heat; simmer, uncovered, 10 minutes. Cool. Cover and refrigerate overnight.

Before serving, strain mint mixture; discard mint. Combine mint liquid, pineapple juice, lemon rind, and juice in a large punch bowl. Slowly pour ginger ale and tonic water into punch. Garnish with additional mint sprigs. Serve immediately. Yield: 1 gallon.

FRUITED CHAMPAGNE PUNCH

6 (16-ounce) cans pitted dark sweet cherries, undrained
3 (12-ounce) cans pineapple juice
1½ cups brandy
1¼ cups lemon juice
6 (25.4-ounce) bottles champagne, chilled

Drain cherries, reserving 2 tablespoons liquid. Combine cherries, pineapple juice, brandy, lemon juice, and reserved cherry liquid in a large punch bowl. Chill thoroughly. To serve, gradually add champagne to punch (do not stir). Serve immediately. Yield: about 6 quarts.

A HOUSEWARMING POTLUCK DINNER

A housewarming party, not exactly a new idea, is a warm and friendly kind of get-together. By 1773, when Philip V. Fithian was tutoring in the Carters' Virginia household, Nomini Hall, he wrote that it was an old custom for any family or person moving into a house or even remodeling one to "Make a Ball and Give a Supper."

Fithian's only problem, when his turn came to have the party, was his inability to dance, a sadness mentioned repeatedly in his diaries. Housewarmings, in our time, have undergone some changes. More often than not, it is the friends of the new occupants of a home who bring in a meal and "Make a Ball."

HOT ARTICHOKE DIP
SAUCY OVEN-BARBECUED CHICKEN
MARINATED VEGETABLE SALAD
SOUR CREAM-MUSTARD POTATO SALAD
CHOCOLATE DELIGHTS
COCONUT POUND CAKE

Serves 10 to 12

Saucy Oven-Barbecued Chicken along with two salads.

Embroidered tableau by Ethel Mohamed of a 1776 housewarming for newlyweds.

HOT ARTICHOKE DIP

2 (14-ounce) cans artichoke
   hearts, drained and chopped
2 cups grated fresh Parmesan
   cheese
2 cups mayonnaise
¼ teaspoon garlic
   salt
Dash of lemon juice

Combine all ingredients, stirring well. Spoon into a lightly greased 1-quart casserole or soufflé dish. Bake at 350° for 20 minutes. Serve hot with crackers. Yield: about 5 cups.

SAUCY OVEN-BARBECUED CHICKEN

1 medium onion, chopped
3 tablespoons bacon
   drippings
1½ cups catsup
1½ cups chicken broth
1½ tablespoons prepared
   mustard
1½ tablespoons vinegar
1½ tablespoons
   Worcestershire sauce
6 whole chicken breasts, split
   and skinned

Sauté onion in bacon drippings in a medium saucepan over low heat until tender. Add catsup, chicken broth, mustard, vinegar, and Worcestershire sauce; stir well. Cook over low heat 15 minutes or until slightly thickened.

Arrange chicken breasts in 13- x 9- x 2-inch baking pans, and pour sauce over chicken. Bake, uncovered, at 350° for 1 hour and 15 minutes or until chicken is tender when pierced with a fork. Baste with barbecue sauce at 15 minute intervals. Yield: 12 servings.

MARINATED VEGETABLE SALAD

1 (1-pound) bunch broccoli
1 medium cauliflower, broken into flowerettes
1 pound carrots, scraped and cut into ½-inch pieces
1 pound fresh mushrooms, sliced
2 small green peppers, cut into 1-inch pieces
8 stalks celery, cut into ½-inch pieces
2 small zucchini, sliced
1 medium cucumber, sliced
3 cups tarragon vinegar
½ cup olive oil
½ cup vegetable oil
½ cup sugar
1 tablespoon prepared mustard
3 cloves garlic, minced
1 tablespoon salt
2 teaspoons dried whole tarragon

Trim off leaves of broccoli; discard tough ends of lower stalks. Cut broccoli into bite-size pieces.

Combine broccoli, cauliflower, carrots, mushrooms, green peppers, celery, zucchini, and cucumber in a large serving bowl; mix well.

Combine vinegar, oil, sugar, mustard, garlic, salt, and tarragon; mix well. Pour over vegetables, and toss well. Cover and refrigerate overnight. Yield: 10 to 12 servings.

SOUR CREAM-MUSTARD POTATO SALAD

10 large new potatoes
8 hard-cooked eggs
2 tablespoons vinegar
2½ tablespoons prepared mustard
1 tablespoon prepared horseradish
1 cup mayonnaise
1 (8-ounce) carton commercial sour cream
1 teaspoon salt
½ teaspoon celery salt
1 cup diced celery
¼ cup finely chopped onion
2 tablespoons chopped green pepper
2 tablespoons chopped pimiento
Cucumber slices (optional)

Cook potatoes in boiling salted water 20 minutes or until potatoes are tender. Drain well, and cool. Peel potatoes, and cut into ½-inch cubes.

Slice eggs in half lengthwise, and carefully remove yolks. Mash yolks in a medium mixing bowl. Add vinegar, mustard, horseradish, mayonnaise, sour cream, salt, and celery salt; mix well. Chop whites, and add to yolk mixture. Add potatoes, celery, onion, green pepper, and pimiento, stirring until well blended. Cover and refrigerate at least 1 hour. Garnish with cucumber slices, if desired. Yield: 10 to 12 servings.

CHOCOLATE DELIGHTS

2 eggs
¾ cup sugar
¼ cup plus 2 tablespoons butter or margarine, melted
2 teaspoons vanilla extract
2 cups chopped pecans
½ cup butter or margarine
1 egg yolk
2 tablespoons water
1¼ cups all-purpose flour
1 teaspoon baking powder
1 teaspoon sugar
1 (12-ounce) package semisweet chocolate morsels

Beat eggs until thick and lemon colored in a small mixing bowl. Add next 4 ingredients; mix well. Set aside.

Combine ½ cup butter, egg yolk, and water; beat until light and fluffy. Add flour, baking powder, and 1 teaspoon sugar; mix well. Press mixture into a lightly greased 13- x 9- x 2-inch baking pan. Bake at 350° for 10 minutes.

Sprinkle chocolate morsels over crust. Return to oven for 1 minute. Remove from oven, and spread melted chocolate evenly over crust using a spatula.

Pour reserved egg mixture over chocolate, spreading evenly. Return to oven, and bake an additional 35 minutes. Cool and cut into 1½-inch squares. Yield: 4 dozen.

COCONUT POUND CAKE

1½ cups butter or margarine, softened
2½ cups sugar
5 eggs
3 cups all-purpose flour
1 teaspoon baking powder
¼ teaspoon salt
1 cup milk
2 teaspoons coconut extract
1 cup flaked coconut

Cream butter; gradually add sugar, and beat at high speed of an electric mixer 10 minutes. Add eggs, one at a time, beating

well after each addition.

Combine flour, baking powder, and salt; add to creamed mixture alternately with milk, beginning and ending with flour mixture. Add coconut extract, beating well. Fold in flaked coconut.

Pour batter into a greased and floured 10-inch tube pan. Place pan in a cold oven. Bake at 300° for 1 hour and 45 minutes. Cool in pan 10 to 15 minutes; remove cake from pan, and cool completely. Yield: one 10-inch cake.

"BURN THE MORTGAGE" OPEN HOUSE

One of the rarest happenings in a mobile society is a "burn the mortgage party." Yet it still happens, and probably more often in the South than in other places. We're mobile, too, but we've still got lots of stay- (and pay-) at-homes. Well, over a term of seemingly endless years of monthly, almost automatic, check writing, there she stands: The homestead. Bought and paid for. Idea: Set aside the price of one more payment, gather your best friends together, and drink a toast as you dispatch the yellowed document with a well-placed match. Make the ceremony as flamboyant as possible; you've earned it! Here's a Southern-style menu that starts with shrimp and could end, early, with Andrew Jackson Coolers, unless you're very cautious.

BOILED SHRIMP WITH RED SAUCE
MEATBALLS IN WINE GRAVY
LAYERED CAVIAR MOLD
ASSORTED CRACKERS AND CHEESES
PEANUT PRALINES
ANDREW JACKSON COOLER
PLANTER'S PUNCH

Serves 12 to 15

Judge J.K.P. Gillaspie and family pose at the homestead. Houston, Texas, c.1915.

Celebrate with Layered Caviar Mold, assorted crackers and cheeses, Planter's Punch, and Andrew Jackson Coolers.

BOILED SHRIMP WITH RED SAUCE

¼ cup plus 2 tablespoons
  catsup
¼ cup plus 2 tablespoons
  chili sauce
¼ cup prepared horseradish
2 teaspoons lemon juice
¼ teaspoon hot sauce
Salt and pepper to taste
About 4 pounds chilled,
  boiled shrimp

Combine all ingredients, except shrimp, stirring until smooth. Cover and chill at least 2 hours. Serve with boiled shrimp. Yield: about 1⅓ cups.

MEATBALLS IN WINE GRAVY

1 pound ground chuck
¾ cup fine dry breadcrumbs
1 small onion, chopped
¼ cup whipping cream
1 egg, beaten
1½ teaspoons salt, divided
¼ cup butter or margarine
¼ cup all-purpose flour
2 cups water
1 cup Burgundy or other dry,
  red wine
¼ teaspoon pepper

Combine ground chuck, breadcrumbs, onion, whipping cream, egg, and 1 teaspoon salt; mix well. Shape mixture into ¾-inch balls. Melt butter in a heavy skillet over low heat. Add meatballs; cook over low heat, turning to brown evenly on all sides. Remove meatballs from skillet; drain.

Add flour to remaining butter in skillet; stir until smooth. Cook 1 minute, stirring constantly. Gradually add water and wine; cook over medium heat, stirring constantly, until thickened and bubbly. Stir in remaining salt and pepper. Add meatballs; simmer, uncovered, 30 minutes. Yield: 3½ dozen.

LAYERED CAVIAR MOLD

2 envelopes unflavored
  gelatin
2 (10¾-ounce) cans chicken
  broth, undiluted and divided
1 (2-ounce) jar red caviar,
  rinsed
2 hard-cooked eggs, chopped
1 (3½-ounce) jar black caviar,
  rinsed
Lettuce leaves (optional)

Soften gelatin in ¼ cup broth; set aside. Place remaining broth in a medium saucepan; bring to a boil. Remove from heat, and add softened gelatin mixture. Cool. Chill until mixture reaches the consistency of unbeaten egg whites. Divide broth mixture into thirds.

Fold red caviar gently into one third, and spoon into a lightly oiled 4-cup mold. Gently fold chopped eggs into one third, and lightly spoon over red caviar mixture. Repeat procedure with black caviar and remaining broth mixture; spoon into mold. Chill until firm.

Unmold onto lettuce-lined platter, if desired, and serve with assorted crackers. Yield: 12 to 15 appetizer servings.

A 1910 postcard congratulating the owners of a new home.

ANDREW JACKSON COOLER

4 ounces champagne
1 ounce gin
1½ teaspoons Simple Syrup
Crushed ice
1½ teaspoons Sparkling
  Burgundy
Orange slice
Maraschino cherry

Combine first 3 ingredients; pour into a 12-ounce serving glass filled with crushed ice. Carefully pour wine over top. Do not stir. Garnish with orange slice and maraschino cherry. Yield: 1 serving.

Simple Syrup:

1 cup sugar
½ cup water

Combine sugar and water in a medium saucepan. Bring to a boil; reduce heat, and simmer 5 minutes. Cool. Yield: ½ cup.

Note: Simple Syrup may be stored in an airtight glass container in the refrigerator.

PLANTER'S PUNCH

¼ cup lime juice
¼ cup orange juice
¼ cup pineapple juice
1 teaspoon grenadine syrup
2 teaspoons sugar
Crushed ice
2 ounces light rum
2 ounces dark Jamaican rum
Orange slice
Pineapple wedge

Combine fruit juices, grenadine syrup, and sugar. Stir until sugar dissolves. Pour into a 12-ounce serving glass filled with crushed ice. Add rum. Garnish with orange slice and pineapple wedge. Yield: 1 serving.

PEANUT PRALINES

2 cups sugar
1 teaspoon baking soda
⅛ teaspoon salt
1 cup buttermilk
1 (12-ounce) can salted
  Spanish peanuts
2 tablespoons butter or
  margarine
1 teaspoon vanilla extract

Combine sugar, baking soda, salt, and buttermilk in a heavy saucepan; mix well. Bring to a boil. Stir in peanuts and butter. Cook over medium heat, stirring occasionally, until mixture reaches soft ball stage (240°).

Remove from heat; add vanilla, and beat with a wooden spoon 2 to 3 minutes or until mixture is creamy and begins to thicken. Working rapidly, drop by rounded tablespoonfuls onto greased waxed paper; let cool. Yield: about 2 dozen.

ONCE IN A LIFETIME

It is not unusual to find, in perusing a family album, the same christening dress being worn by babies of three or even four generations. A youngster staring at a picture of his grandfather as an infant in a little white gown will remind us that baby pictures, unlabeled, can be rather anonymous-looking. How we wish someone had put names and dates to those ancestral photographs of ours!

The christening gown represents a continuum, one of the precious handed-down heirlooms of the Southern family. It reflects, too, the first of several one-of-a-kind moments in a given life, the sort of events we celebrate in this chapter.

Food sharing has been a part of ceremonies of all kinds since history began. Our menus will take us from the brunch that follows a morning christening in a Catholic church through a luncheon enjoyed by a Jewish congregation at a boy's bar mitzvah, and will see us through our wedding-related galas.

The South has always fancied weddings. We start celebrating the moment the engagement is announced, planning the gifts and parties. In this chapter we look at some things that have changed: The wedding gown, for example, once any beautiful, becoming color, is now "traditionally" white or ivory. And some things that have not changed: Our wedding breakfast is not much different now from the way it was in the social heyday of Andrew Jackson's graceful Hermitage, scene of so many such parties.

The wedding reception was always held at home in the early days when there were no clubs, ballrooms, or other likely places for large parties. Whenever we can do so, we adhere to the old custom, filling the home with flowers and happy people.

Some customs have mercifully evaporated. Before the turn of the century, the wedding party lasted all night. In the rural South, the women would put the bride to bed; then the men would install the groom beside her. After which, dancing and revelry were kept going all night, with as much noise as could be made by all present. Our receptions are of shorter duration now. But our reception food is similar to the old-time "supper" served late in the evening before and during the night-long dancing and spiritous conviviality.

MENU OF MENUS

CHRISTENING DAY
BRUNCH

A BAR MITZVAH
LUNCHEON

GRADUATION BUFFET

BRIDESMAIDS PINK
LUNCHEON

JUNE BRIDAL LUNCHEON

WEDDING BREAKFAST AT
THE HERMITAGE

WEDDING RECEPTION AT
HOME

CHRISTENING DAY BRUNCH

hristening, the ancient sacrament of the Christian church, means to make Christian and represents the grace that removes original sin, an essential to salvation. The protection of the Holy Trinity is invoked by the officiating minister. Roman Catholic, orthodox, and Anglican christenings require that the baby have a sponsor, a godmother and/or godfather. The naming of the child is secondary to the religious aspect of the sacrament. Since the ceremony takes place at a morning service, the christening party frequently adjourns to a brunch given by a family member. This menu is light but satisfying and ends with a champagne toast to the baby.

TOMATO SOUP
FRESH VEGETABLE BOWL
CONGEALED VEAL LOAF
WHOLE WHEAT ANGEL BISCUITS
VANILLA CRESCENTS * APRICOT BALLS
CHAMPAGNE

Serves 8

A 1909 postcard proudly announces, "It's a boy."

TOMATO SOUP

5 tomatoes, peeled and sliced
2 medium onions, sliced
1 to 2 tablespoons sugar
1 sprig fresh parsley
1 teaspoon salt
⅛ teaspoon pepper
½ teaspoon Worcestershire sauce
2 tablespoons cornstarch
¾ cup water
2 tablespoons plain yogurt (optional)

Combine tomatoes, onion, sugar, parsley, salt, pepper, and Worcestershire sauce in a medium Dutch oven. Cover and cook over medium heat 20 minutes or until vegetables are tender.

Process tomato mixture through a food mill. Return tomato mixture to Dutch oven; discard pulp.

Combine cornstarch and water, stirring until smooth; add to tomato mixture, stirring well. Bring to a boil; reduce heat, and simmer until soup is thickened. Serve soup hot or chilled; garnish each serving with 1 teaspoon plain yogurt, if desired. Yield: 4 cups.

FRESH VEGETABLE BOWL

1 pound fresh green beans, cleaned
1 pound fresh carrots, scraped and cut into 3-inch pieces
1 pound fresh brussels sprouts, cleaned
1 pound cauliflower flowerets
1 pound fresh mushrooms, sliced
Garlic-Mayonnaise Dip

Arrange green beans, carrots, brussels sprouts, cauliflower, and mushrooms in a steaming rack. Place over boiling water; cover and steam 10 minutes or to desired degree of doneness. Chill vegetables.

Arrange chilled vegetables on a serving platter. Serve with Garlic-Mayonnaise Dip. Yield: 24 servings.

Garlic-Mayonnaise Dip:

2 egg yolks
1 teaspoon salt
½ teaspoon dry mustard
¼ teaspoon paprika
Dash of red pepper
2 tablespoons vinegar
2 cups vegetable oil
2 tablespoons lemon juice
1 tablespoon hot water
2 cloves garlic, sliced

Allow egg yolks to reach room temperature.

Combine salt, mustard, paprika, and pepper in a small mixing bowl. Add yolks; beat at medium-high speed of an electric mixer 1 to 2 minutes or until thickened. Add vinegar; beat an additional 30 seconds.

Add ¼ cup oil, one drop at a time, to yolk mixture, beating constantly at medium-high speed of an electric mixer. Be sure that oil is thoroughly combined in egg yolk mixture before adding another drop.

Add 1¼ cups oil, 1 tablespoon at a time, being sure oil is thoroughly combined in yolk mixture before adding another tablespoon. Scrape mixing bowl frequently during entire procedure. Add remaining ½ cup oil alternately with lemon juice and water, beating constantly.

Spoon mixture into a serving bowl. Add garlic. Cover and refrigerate overnight. Remove garlic slices and discard. Stir mixture before serving. Yield: about 2 cups.

CONGEALED VEAL LOAF

1 pound boneless veal cutlets
1 pound boneless pork steaks
1 large onion, sliced
3 cups water
1 teaspoon salt
2 envelopes unflavored gelatin
½ cup water
1 cup mayonnaise
3 hard-cooked eggs, chopped
3 tablespoons vinegar
2 tablespoons prepared mustard
1 tablespoon sugar
2 teaspoons salt
¼ teaspoon pepper
Lettuce leaves
Fresh parsley sprigs
Carrot flowers

Combine veal, pork, onion, 3 cups water, and 1 teaspoon salt in a large saucepan. Bring to a boil. Reduce heat; cover and simmer 1 hour or until meat is very tender. Remove meat from broth; set aside to cool. Reserve broth in saucepan. Simmer until broth is reduced to 1 cup. Set broth aside.

Position knife blade in food processor bowl; add meat. Process 3 to 5 seconds. Scrape sides of bowl with a rubber spatula. Process 3 to 5 additional seconds or until meat is ground. Remove meat to a large mixing bowl. Set aside.

Soften gelatin in ½ cup water. Stir into broth. Bring to a boil; cook 1 to 2 minutes. Set aside.

Add mayonnaise, eggs, vinegar, mustard, sugar, 2 teaspoons salt, pepper, and broth mixture to ground meat in mixing bowl; stir well. Spoon into a lightly greased 8½- x 4½- x 3-inch loafpan. Cover and chill overnight. Unmold onto a lettuce-lined serving plate. Garnish with parsley and carrot flowers. Yield: 8 servings.

Virginia Historical Society

WHOLE WHEAT ANGEL BISCUITS

1 package dry yeast
½ teaspoon sugar
2 tablespoons warm water (105° to 115°)
3½ cups all-purpose flour, divided
1½ cups whole wheat flour
¼ cup sugar
1 tablespoon baking powder
1 teaspoon baking soda
1 teaspoon salt
1 cup shortening
2 cups plus 2 tablespoons warm buttermilk (105° to 115°)

Dissolve yeast and ½ teaspoon sugar in warm water; let stand 5 minutes or until bubbly.

Combine 1½ cups all-purpose flour, wheat flour, ¼ cup sugar, baking powder, soda, and salt in a large mixing bowl. Cut in shortening with a pastry blender until mixture resembles coarse meal. Add yeast mixture and buttermilk, stirring until dry ingredients are moistened. Stir in enough remaining all-purpose flour to make a soft dough.

Turn dough out onto a lightly floured surface, and knead 4 to 5 times or until dough is smooth and elastic. Let dough rest 10 minutes.

Roll dough to ¼-inch thickness; cut with a 2-inch biscuit cutter, and place on lightly greased baking sheets. Bake at 400° for 10 to 12 minutes. Yield: about 5½ dozen.

VANILLA CRESCENTS

1 cup sifted powdered
  sugar
1 vanilla bean, grated
2¾ cups sifted cake flour
⅔ cup ground blanched
  almonds
¼ cup sugar
1 teaspoon vanilla extract
1 cup butter, softened
½ cup cold water

Combine powdered sugar and vanilla bean, stirring well. Cover and let stand 24 hours.

Combine flour, almonds, sugar, and vanilla extract in a medium mixing bowl; cut in butter with a pastry blender until mixture resembles coarse meal. Sprinkle cold water, 1 tablespoon at a time, evenly over surface; stir with a fork until dry ingredients are moistened. Shape dough into a ball; chill at least 45 minutes.

Divide dough into 1-inch balls; shape each ball into a crescent-shaped cookie. Place on ungreased baking sheets. Bake at 350° for 15 minutes or until lightly browned. Cool on wire racks. Roll cookies in reserved powdered sugar mixture. Yield: about 4 dozen.

Ethel Wright Mohamed's embroidered picture welcomes a new baby.

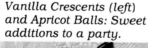

Vanilla Crescents (left) and Apricot Balls: Sweet additions to a party.

APRICOT BALLS

3 (6-ounce) packages dried
  apricots, finely chopped
2 cups sugar
3 tablespoons grated orange
  rind
⅔ cup orange juice
1 cup sifted powdered sugar
Pecan halves

Combine apricots, 2 cups sugar, orange rind, and juice in a large saucepan. Bring to a boil; reduce heat, and simmer 25 minutes or until liquid is absorbed, stirring frequently. Remove from heat, and cool completely.

Drop mixture by teaspoonfuls onto waxed paper, and allow to dry at room temperature 1 hour. Shape mixture into balls, and roll in powdered sugar. Press a pecan half into each ball. Yield: about 6 dozen.

Note: Apricot Balls are best when prepared one day before serving so that they can dry overnight. A food processor may be used to finely chop apricots.

A BAR MITZVAH LUNCHEON

At age thirteen, a Jewish boy attains the age of religious duty and responsibility. The ceremony held at his synagogue recognizes the boy as a bar mitzvah which means son of the (divine) law. A girl becomes bas mitzvah at thirteen. A Kentucky-style bar mitzvah surprised a woman who moved down from the North: Instead of the mother doing all the baking, the women of the synagogue helped, each baking her specialty. And in Kentucky, the boy's family gives a lavish "dairy" luncheon for the congregation after the ceremony that would include no meat. Lox, noodle kugel, a lavish platter of freshly cut fruit sprinkled with cocoriva, a coconut liqueur . . . a few of the good things one eats at a bar mitzvah celebration. An extravagant private supper may take place that evening. Bar mitzvah time is joyous and meaningful.

SMOKED SALMON MOLD WITH BAGELS
EGG SALAD
NOODLE KUGEL
SEVEN-LAYER CONGEALED VEGETABLE SALAD
LEMON BARS
BAR MITZVAH BROWNIES
FRUIT STRUDEL
BAR MITZVAH CAKE

Serves 8 to 10

SMOKED SALMON MOLD WITH BAGELS

2 (8-ounce) packages cream cheese, softened
½ pound smoked salmon fillets (lox)
Dash of seasoned salt
Dash of onion powder
Lettuce leaves
10 Bagels

Combine cheese and salmon in a mixing bowl; beat until smooth. Add salt and onion powder; beat until well blended.

Lightly oil a 2½-cup fish mold, and line with plastic wrap. Spoon mixture into mold; chill several hours. Turn out onto a lettuce-lined serving dish, and peel off plastic wrap. Serve with bagels. Yield: 8 to 10 servings.

EGG SALAD

24 hard-cooked eggs, chopped
2 cups finely chopped celery
1 cup mayonnaise
2 tablespoons finely chopped onion
2 tablespoons lemon juice
2 teaspoons salt
½ teaspoon white pepper
Lettuce leaves
Green pepper rings (optional)

Combine eggs, celery, mayonnaise, onion, lemon juice, salt, and pepper in a large mixing bowl; stir until well blended. Cover and chill.

Serve egg salad on lettuce leaves; garnish with green pepper rings, if desired. Yield: 8 to 10 servings.

NOODLE KUGEL

½ cup butter or margarine, melted and divided
1 (12-ounce) package medium-size egg noodles
⅓ cup sugar
¼ teaspoon salt
3 medium apples, peeled and grated
3 eggs, beaten
1 (8-ounce) carton commercial sour cream
1 cup cottage cheese
1 cup orange juice
2 cups crushed cornflakes

Spread ¼ cup melted butter in the bottom of a 13- x 9- x 2-inch baking dish; set aside.

Prepare noodles according to package directions; drain. Combine noodles, sugar, salt, apples, eggs, sour cream, cottage cheese, and orange juice in a large bowl, stirring well. Spoon mixture into baking dish. Combine cornflakes and remaining butter; sprinkle over noodle mixture.

Bake at 325° for 1½ hours. Serve immediately. Yield: 8 to 10 servings.

Seven-Layer Salad (front) with salad dressing and Egg Salad garnished with green pepper rings.

SEVEN-LAYER CONGEALED VEGETABLE SALAD

1 (16-ounce) can diced beets, undrained
2 envelopes unflavored gelatin
½ cup cold water
1 cup boiling water
½ cup vinegar
1 teaspoon lemon juice
½ teaspoon Worcestershire sauce
⅛ teaspoon hot sauce
4 hard-cooked eggs, chopped
1 (17-ounce) can green peas, drained
1 (3¼-ounce) jar cocktail onions, drained
1 cup chopped celery
1 (16-ounce) can French-style green beans, drained
Lettuce leaves
Dressing (recipe follows)

Drain beets, reserving liquid; set beets aside. Add water to beet liquid to equal 2 cups; set liquid aside.

Soften gelatin in ½ cup cold water. Add boiling water, and stir until gelatin dissolves. Add reserved beet liquid mixture, vinegar, lemon juice, Worcestershire sauce, and hot sauce, stirring well; chill 1 hour.

Sprinkle chopped eggs evenly in the bottom of a lightly oiled 9-cup mold. Layer diced beets, green peas, onions, celery, and green beans over eggs. Pour gelatin mixture over vegetables. Chill until firm. Unmold onto a lettuce-lined plate. Slice and serve with dressing. Yield: 8 to 10 servings.

Dressing:

1 cup mayonnaise
¼ cup crumbled blue cheese
2 tablespoons lemon juice

Combine mayonnaise, cheese, and lemon juice, stirring until well blended. Yield: about 1¼ cups.

LEMON BARS

1 cup butter or margarine, softened
½ cup sifted powdered sugar
2 cups all-purpose flour
4 eggs
1¾ cups sugar
¼ cup all-purpose flour
1 teaspoon baking powder
½ teaspoon salt
2 teaspoons grated lemon rind
½ cup lemon juice
Additional powdered sugar

Cream butter and ½ cup powdered sugar; add 2 cups flour, beating well. Press pastry into a lightly greased 15- x 10- x 1-inch jellyroll pan. Bake at 350° for 15 minutes or until lightly browned.

Combine eggs and sugar; beat well. Add ¼ cup flour, baking powder, salt, lemon rind, and juice, beating well. Pour over baked crust.

Bake at 350° for 25 minutes or until lightly browned. Let cool, and cut into 1½-inch squares. Sprinkle with additional powdered sugar. Yield: about 5 dozen.

BAR MITZVAH BROWNIES

1 cup butter or margarine,
  softened
1¾ cups sugar
4 eggs
4 (1-ounce) squares
  unsweetened chocolate,
  melted
1¾ cups all-purpose flour
1 teaspoon baking powder
½ cup bourbon
2 teaspoons vanilla extract
1 cup chopped black walnuts
  or pecans
Chocolate-Bourbon Frosting

Cream butter; gradually add
sugar, beating until light and
fluffy. Add eggs, one at a time,
beating well after each addition.
Add melted chocolate, and beat
until blended.

Combine flour and baking
powder; add to chocolate mixture alternately with bourbon,
beginning and ending with
flour mixture. Stir in vanilla
and desired nuts. Pour batter
into a greased 13- x 9- x 2-inch
baking pan.

Bake at 350° for 25 minutes.
Cool brownies completely.
Spread with Chocolate-Bourbon
Frosting. Cut into squares.
Yield: about 2 dozen.

Chocolate-Bourbon Frosting:

1 egg, beaten
3 tablespoons bourbon
1 teaspoon lemon juice
1 teaspoon vanilla extract
¼ cup butter or margarine
2 (1-ounce) squares
  unsweetened chocolate,
  melted
2½ cups sifted powdered
  sugar

Combine egg, bourbon, lemon
juice, and vanilla in a small mixing bowl; stir until well blended.
Set aside.

Cream butter in a medium
mixing bowl; add chocolate, and
beat until blended. Gradually
add sugar to chocolate mixture
alternately with bourbon mixture, beating until mixture is
smooth. Yield: frosting for one
13- x 9-inch cake.

Louis Schmier, *Binding Ties: A Photographic Glimpse of the Jewish Experience in Georgia*, Creative Concepts Press, Marietta, Georgia, 1984

William Landey, Valdosta, Georgia, at his Bar Mitzvah, 1906.

FRUIT STRUDEL

5 cups all-purpose flour
2 tablespoons sugar
½ teaspoon salt
¾ cup plus 2 tablespoons warm water (105° to 115°)
¾ cup plus 2 tablespoons warm vegetable oil (105° to 115°)
3 eggs, beaten
1 (15-ounce) package golden raisins, finely minced
2 (8-ounce) packages dried apricots, finely minced
2 (7-ounce) cans flaked coconut
1 lemon, seeded and finely minced
1 orange, seeded and finely minced
1 (16-ounce) jar red maraschino cherries, drained and finely minced
2 cups crushed cornflakes
2 (10-ounce) jars apricot preserves
1 (16-ounce) jar peach preserves
1 (20-ounce) can crushed pineapple, drained
Vegetable oil
3 tablespoons ground cinnamon
¼ cup sugar
1¾ cups coarsely chopped pecans, divided
Sifted powdered sugar

Combine flour, 2 tablespoons sugar, and salt in a large mixing bowl; mix well. Make a well in center of mixture. Combine water and oil; add to dry ingredients, mixing well. Add eggs; mix well. Turn dough out onto a floured surface, and knead 5 minutes or until dough is smooth and elastic. Cover dough with a warm bowl, and let rest 30 minutes.

Combine next 7 ingredients in a large mixing bowl, mixing well. Add preserves and pineapple; mix well. Set aside.

Divide dough into 7 equal portions. Roll 1 portion into a 15- x 10-inch rectangle, rolling as thin as possible without tearing. Brush surface of dough with oil. Combine cinnamon and ¼ cup sugar; sprinkle 2 teaspoons sugar mixture evenly over surface of dough. Set remaining sugar mixture aside.

Spread 1½ cups fruit mixture along wide end of dough, leaving a 1-inch margin along outside edges. Sprinkle ¼ cup pecans over fruit mixture.

Starting at wide end, roll up jellyroll fashion, turning edges under. Pinch seams together to seal. Place on a well-greased baking sheet; brush top with oil. Sprinkle lightly with reserved sugar mixture. Repeat procedure with remaining portions of dough.

Bake at 350° for 30 minutes or until lightly browned. Remove from baking sheets and cool on wire racks. Cut into 1-inch pieces, and sprinkle with powdered sugar. Yield: 7 loaves.

I n Kentucky synagogues, a separate table is given over to cheesecakes. The baker especially famous for her cheesecakes is put in charge of serving them. Two honored older women are invited to preside at silver coffee and tea services at opposite ends of the table. There are always many sweets, including the exquisite strudel. The traditional food is not "Southern"; it is middle European.

BAR MITZVAH CAKE

1 cup butter or margarine, softened
2 cups sugar
4 eggs, separated
3 cups all-purpose flour
2 teaspoons baking powder
¼ teaspoon salt
1 cup milk
1 tablespoon vanilla extract
Frosting (recipe follows)
Blue paste food coloring

Cream butter; gradually add sugar, beating well. Add egg yolks, one at a time, beating well after each addition.

Combine flour, baking powder, and salt; add to creamed mixture alternately with milk, beginning and ending with flour mixture. Stir in vanilla.

Beat egg whites (at room temperature) until stiff peaks form; fold into batter.

Spoon batter into a greased and floured 13½- x 9½-inch book-shaped cakepan. Bake at 350° for 35 minutes or until a wooden pick inserted in center comes out clean. Cool cake in pan 10 minutes; remove from pan, and let cool completely.

Spread frosting on top and sides of cake, reserving ½ cup frosting. Tint reserved frosting bright blue. Spoon tinted frosting into a pastry bag. Pipe a Star of David and desired inscription on top of cake. Yield: one 13½- x 9½-inch book cake.

Frosting:

¼ cup plus 2 tablespoons butter or margarine, softened
4 cups sifted powdered sugar
2 egg whites
1 teaspoon almond extract
1 to 2 teaspoons milk

Cream butter in a large mixing bowl. Gradually add sugar alternately with egg whites; beat mixture well after each addition. Beat in almond extract. Stir in milk as needed for spreading consistency. Yield: frosting for one 13½- x 9½-inch book cake.

GRADUATION BUFFET LUNCHEON

There have been changes in Southern education since the days when children of the wealthy were tutored at home, and then sent to Europe to round out their training, while others less fortunate were lucky to be taught to read and write. Aspiring students in the early 1900s, unless they lived in a college town, had to leave home after sketchy preparation. Girls might go to finishing school or "normal school," while boys "read" law or otherwise followed their ambitions. Standardized education at the secondary level has given us a better-educated South, with more young people able to make an informed choice as to trying college. Senior year in high school, before the solemn young pick up their diplomas, is fraught with class trips, picnics, proms, and, for some lucky ones, a lovely luncheon like this.

SHRIMP AND CRABMEAT MOUSSE
CHILLED STEAMED ASPARAGUS
CREAMED CHICKEN IN PATTY SHELLS
RUM PUDDING WITH BLACKBERRY SAUCE

Serves 8

A graduating class boats with friends at Oxford Lake Park, Anniston, Alabama, 1890.

The graduating class of the Home Institute, a New Orleans boarding school, 1898.

SHRIMP AND CRABMEAT MOUSSE

1½ cups tomato juice
1 (8-ounce) package cream
　cheese, softened
1 tablespoon onion juice
1 teaspoon lemon juice
¼ teaspoon salt
¼ teaspoon hot sauce
2 envelopes unflavored
　gelatin
¼ cup cold water
2 cups cooked, chopped
　shrimp
1 cup lump crabmeat
1 small green pepper,
　chopped
½ cup mayonnaise
½ cup sliced pimiento-stuffed
　olives
¼ cup chopped celery
2 tablespoons chopped
　pimiento
½ cup whipping cream,
　whipped
Lettuce leaves
Chilled Steamed Asparagus
(optional)

Combine tomato juice, cream cheese, onion juice, lemon juice, salt, and hot sauce in top of a double boiler. Cook over boiling water until cheese melts, stirring constantly.

Dissolve gelatin in cold water; add to tomato juice mixture, stirring well. Remove from heat; cool. Add shrimp, crabmeat, green pepper, mayonnaise, olives, celery, and pimiento; mixing well. Gently fold in whipped cream.

Pour mixture into an oiled 5½-cup fish mold; chill several hours or overnight. Unmold onto a lettuce-lined serving plate. Serve as a salad with Chilled Steamed Asparagus, if desired. Yield: 8 servings.

CHILLED STEAMED ASPARAGUS

1½ pounds fresh asparagus
　spears

Snap off tough ends of asparagus. Remove scales from stalks with a knife or vegetable peeler, if desired. Tie asparagus into a bundle with string. Stand bundle, tips up, in bottom of a double boiler. Add boiling water to fill pan half full. Cover with top of double boiler turned upside down for a lid. Simmer 10 minutes or until asparagus is crisp-tender. Drain and refresh quickly by running asparagus under cold water to retain color. Chill thoroughly before serving. Yield: 8 servings.

CREAMED CHICKEN IN PATTY SHELLS

1 cup sliced fresh
  mushrooms
¼ cup finely chopped green
  pepper
½ cup butter or margarine,
  divided
½ cup all-purpose flour
1 cup milk
1 cup chicken broth
2 cups diced cooked chicken
¼ cup chopped pimiento
2 egg yolks
2 tablespoons lemon juice
¼ teaspoon prepared mustard
1 teaspoon salt
1 teaspoon paprika
8 commercial patty shells,
  baked

Sauté mushrooms and green pepper in 2 tablespoons butter in a small saucepan until tender. Set aside.

Melt remaining butter in a heavy saucepan over low heat; add flour, and stir until smooth. Cook 1 minute, stirring constantly. Combine milk and chicken broth; gradually add to flour mixture, stirring constantly. Cook over medium heat, stirring constantly, until thickened and bubbly. Stir in sautéed vegetables, chicken, and pimiento.

Beat yolks. Gradually stir one-fourth hot mixture into yolks; add to remaining hot mixture, stirring constantly.

Combine remaining ingredients, except patty shells; stir into creamed mixture. Bring to a boil; reduce heat, and simmer 10 minutes. Spoon mixture into patty shells. Serve immediately. Yield: 8 servings.

An intriguing flavor blend to top off a graduation luncheon: Rum Pudding with Blackberry Sauce.

RUM PUDDING WITH BLACKBERRY SAUCE

3 egg yolks
¼ cup plus 2 tablespoons
  sugar
2 tablespoons dark rum
1 teaspoon vanilla extract
¼ teaspoon salt
1 envelope unflavored gelatin
¾ cup cold water
1 cup whipping cream
Blackberry Sauce

Beat yolks in a medium mixing bowl until thick and lemon colored. Gradually add sugar, beating well. Add rum, vanilla, and salt, beating well.

Soften gelatin in cold water in a saucepan. Bring to a boil, stirring until gelatin dissolves. Cool slightly. Slowly pour gelatin into rum mixture; beat constantly. Cool completely.

Beat whipping cream until soft peaks form. Fold into rum mixture. Pour into a lightly oiled 4-cup mold, and chill until set. Unmold pudding onto a serving platter. Spoon Blackberry Sauce over pudding. Yield: 8 servings.

Blackberry Sauce:

1 (16-ounce) package frozen
  blackberries, thawed
½ cup sugar
1 tablespoon cornstarch

Combine blackberries and sugar in a saucepan; bring to a boil, and boil 5 minutes. Process mixture through a food mill. Combine a small amount of hot blackberry mixture and cornstarch; stir into remaining blackberry mixture. Cook over low heat, stirring constantly, until smooth and thickened. Cool. Yield: 1 cup.

BRIDESMAIDS PINK LUNCHEON

Marion Harland in *Breakfast, Luncheon and Tea*, 1877, has an illuminating anecdote on the term "luncheon." A young woman was horrified when her brother turned up with three unexpected dinner guests. She washed her hands of the situation. "Any pie or cake in the house," he said. "Any fruit, fresh or preserved?" "Yes, but it isn't a question of dessert. There is nothing for dinner!" "I understand. I have it," he cried. He asked her to put out all her good pantry things, the desserts, wine, and coffee, and "Call it luncheon!" Luncheon is a perfect entertainment for bridesmaids. This one's frilly, feminine, and frankly pink.

CRANBERRY JUICE COCKTAIL
SHRIMP IN CARDINAL SAUCE
INDIVIDUAL TOMATO ASPICS
CRESCENT ROLLS
STRAWBERRY DELIGHT

Serves 8

CRANBERRY JUICE COCKTAIL

2 (12-ounce) packages fresh
  cranberries
2 quarts water
Cheesecloth
1⅓ cups sugar
Juice of 2 lemons
6 whole cloves

Combine cranberries and water in a Dutch oven; bring to a boil. Cover and cook 10 minutes or until berries pop open. Strain mixture through very fine cheesecloth. Discard pulp.

Return strained juice to Dutch oven; add sugar, lemon juice, and cloves. Boil 5 minutes. Remove cloves, and discard. Chill juice thoroughly. Serve cold. Yield: about 8 cups.

Spice label, 1800s

SHRIMP IN CARDINAL SAUCE

¼ cup butter or margarine
¼ cup all-purpose flour
2 cups whipping cream
1 tablespoon tomato paste
1 teaspoon salt
½ teaspoon garlic salt
¼ teaspoon curry powder
¼ teaspoon ground ginger
Dash of hot sauce
3 cups cooked small shrimp,
  peeled and deveined
2 teaspoons brandy (optional)
Additional cooked small
  shrimp
Fresh parsley sprigs

Melt butter in a medium saucepan over low heat; add flour, stirring until smooth. Cook 1 minute, stirring constantly. Gradually add whipping cream; cook over medium heat, stirring constantly, until mixture is thickened and bubbly.

Stir in tomato paste; blend well. Add salt, garlic salt, curry powder, ginger, and hot sauce, mixing well. Stir in 3 cups shrimp and brandy, if desired. Spoon mixture into 8 scallop shells or ramekins. Bake at 350° for 15 minutes. Garnish with additional shrimp and parsley. Yield: 8 servings.

A treasure from a family album: This little girl was a member of a wedding party in Georgia, c.1900.

INDIVIDUAL TOMATO ASPICS

1 (28-ounce) can whole tomatoes, undrained
4 stalks celery with leaves, cut in half
3 tablespoons chopped onion
2 tablespoons lemon juice
1 bay leaf
1 teaspoon salt
½ teaspoon paprika
3 envelopes unflavored gelatin
1 (24-ounce) can vegetable cocktail juice, divided
1 (8-ounce) can artichoke hearts, drained and chopped
1 (8-ounce) can sliced water chestnuts, drained and chopped
1 hard-cooked egg, chopped
½ cup finely chopped celery
¼ cup finely chopped green pepper
1½ tablespoons finely chopped pimiento-stuffed olives
Lettuce leaves
Mayonnaise

Combine tomatoes, celery stalks, onion, lemon juice, bay leaf, salt, and paprika in a large, heavy saucepan. Cover and cook over medium heat 15 minutes. Strain mixture, reserving tomato juice and discarding vegetables and bay leaf. Return tomato juice to saucepan.

Dissolve gelatin in ½ cup vegetable cocktail juice, stirring well. Add gelatin mixture to tomato juice in saucepan. Add additional vegetable cocktail juice to yield 4 cups. Chill until mixture reaches the consistency of unbeaten egg whites.

Fold in artichoke hearts, water chestnuts, egg, celery, green pepper, and olives. Pour mixture evenly into 8 lightly oiled ½-cup heart-shaped molds. Refrigerate until firm.

Unmold aspics onto individual lettuce-lined salad plates; garnish each with a dollop of mayonnaise. Yield: 8 servings.

All is pink, from Shrimp in Cardinal Sauce and Tomato Aspic to Strawberry Delight.

CRESCENT ROLLS

1 package dry yeast
1 cup warm water (105° to 115°), divided
¼ cup sugar
½ cup shortening
1¼ teaspoons salt
3 eggs, beaten
5 cups all-purpose flour
¼ cup butter or margarine, melted and divided

Dissolve yeast in 2 tablespoons warm water; stir well. Let stand 5 minutes or until bubbly.

Combine remaining water, sugar, shortening, and salt in a large mixing bowl; stir until shortening melts. Add dissolved yeast and eggs; mix well. Stir in flour to make a soft dough.

Turn dough out onto a lightly floured surface; knead 10 minutes or until dough is smooth and elastic. Place dough in a greased bowl, turning to grease top. Cover and let rise in a warm place (85°), free from drafts, 1½ hours or until doubled in bulk. Punch dough down; turn out onto a floured surface. Knead an additional 10 minutes.

Divide dough into four equal portions. Roll each portion into a circle 12 inches in diameter and ¼-inch thick; brush with melted butter. Cut each circle into 12 wedges; roll each wedge tightly, beginning at wide end.

Place rolls on greased baking sheets, point side down; curve into crescent shape. Brush with remaining melted butter. Cover and let rise in a warm place (85°), free from drafts, 1 hour or until doubled in bulk. Bake at 375° for 20 minutes or until lightly browned. Yield: 4 dozen.

Note: Crescent Rolls may be baked ahead of time and frozen for later use.

STRAWBERRY DELIGHT

2 egg whites
1 cup sugar
2 cups whipping cream, whipped
2 pints fresh stawberries, washed, hulled, drained, and sliced
2 (3-ounce) packages lady fingers

Beat egg whites (at room temperature) in a large mixing bowl until foamy. Gradually add sugar, 1 tablespoon at a time, beating until stiff peaks form. Gently fold whipped cream into beaten egg whites.

Set aside ¼ cup sliced strawberries for garnish. Fold remaining strawberries into whipped cream mixture.

Cut lady fingers in half crosswise. Line 8 individual serving dishes with lady finger halves. Spoon strawberry mixture evenly into each dish; garnish with sliced strawberries. Chill. Yield: 8 servings.

JUNE BRIDAL LUNCHEON

The bridal luncheon is a relative newcomer to society since the days of Colonial Williamsburg. A white wedding dress and veil were not mandatory then, and a wedding was often planned to coincide with the holiday season when reunions were in full swing. Families came home and held one long house party, with feasting, drinking, and dancing. It was not until cities grew and transportation became easier that the modern bridal party, often held at one's club, became possible. This luncheon is typical of many served at the Centennial Club in Nashville in the 1950s.

CANTALOUPE LILIES WITH MELON BALLS
BAKED CHICKEN WITH
WINE AND MUSHROOMS
CONFETTI RICE
ASPARAGUS WITH LEMON BUTTER
PALE GREEN MERINGUE HEARTS WITH
PASTEL SHERBETS

Serves 8

Attendants at the Atlanta wedding of John S. Spalding and Mary Connally, 1902.

CANTALOUPE LILIES WITH MELON BALLS

1 large honeydew, halved and
   seeded
4 small cantaloupes
1½ pounds seedless red
   grapes
1½ pounds seedless white
   grapes
3 egg whites, slightly beaten
2½ cups sugar

Scoop out honeydew balls, and set aside. Discard honeydew shell.

Cut a thin slice from both ends of each cantaloupe. Draw V-shaped sections around melons with a sharp pencil, being sure to stop the pointed ends 1½ inches from the top and bottom. Using a sharp paring knife, cut through melon along lines drawn. Gently pull melon halves apart; remove and discard seeds and pulp. Slice rind away from melon, stopping at base of the V. Gently press rind down, leaving melon standing intact. Fill cantaloupe lilies with honeydew balls; chill.

Divide grapes into small bunches; dip each bunch in egg whites, and place on a wire rack. Sprinkle generously with sugar. Allow grapes to dry at least 2½ hours in a cool place (do not refrigerate).

Serve filled cantaloupe lilies with white and red frosted grapes. Yield: 8 servings.

A first course pleasing to eye and palate: Cantaloupe Lilies filled with melon balls and garnished with seedless red and white grapes that have been sugared and dried.

BAKED CHICKEN WITH WINE AND MUSHROOMS

4 whole chicken breasts,
   split, boned, and skinned
½ teaspoon salt
¼ teaspoon pepper
½ cup butter or margarine,
   melted
½ cup chopped shallots
½ cup Chablis or other dry,
   white wine
½ pound fresh mushrooms,
   sliced
2 tablespoons chopped fresh
   parsley

Sprinkle surface of chicken with salt and pepper; brown on all sides in butter in a large skillet. Remove chicken from skillet, and set aside.

Sauté shallots in butter in skillet until tender. Return chicken breasts to skillet; add wine. Cover and cook over low heat 20 minutes. Add mushrooms and chopped parsley; cover and continue cooking 5 minutes or until chicken is tender. Remove chicken to a warm serving platter; spoon mushroom sauce over chicken and serve. Yield: 8 servings.

CONFETTI RICE

1 (10-ounce) package frozen
   green peas
2 cups cooked rice
2 tablespoons chopped
   pimiento
⅔ cup vegetable oil
3 tablespoons vinegar
½ teaspoon salt
¼ teaspoon sugar
¼ teaspoon dried whole basil
Lettuce leaves (optional)

Cook peas according to package directions; drain. Combine peas, rice, and pimiento in a medium mixing bowl; stir well.

Combine oil, vinegar, salt, sugar, and basil, stirring well. Pour over rice mixture, gently tossing to combine. Drain salad; cover and refrigerate several hours before serving. Serve on lettuce leaves, if desired. Yield: 8 servings.

Centennial Club members
pose, in 1922, on the steps of
the club, a favorite setting
for Nashville luncheon parties.

The pre-nuptial preliminaries of an antebellum Virginia wedding were remembered like this by Letitia M. Burwell: "The preparations usually commenced some time before, with saving eggs, butter, chickens, etc.; after which ensued the liveliest eggbeating, butter creaming, raisinstoning, sugar-pounding, cake-icing, coconut-grating, egg-frothing, wafer making, jelly-straining, silver cleaning, dress making, lacewashing, ruffle crimping, tarlatan-smoothing, trunk moving, guests arriving, servants running, girls laughing! . . ."

From *A Girl's Life in Virginia Before the War*

ASPARAGUS WITH LEMON BUTTER

2 pounds fresh asparagus
  spears
½ cup butter, melted
3 tablespoons lemon juice

Snap off tough ends of asparagus. Remove scales from stalks with a knife or vegetable peeler, if desired. Tie asparagus into a bundle with string.

Stand bundle, tips up, in bottom of a double boiler. Add boiling water to fill pan half full. Cover with top of double boiler turned upside down. Simmer until crisp-tender; drain. Place asparagus on a serving platter. Cut and discard string.

Combine butter and lemon juice; pour over asparagus. Serve hot. Yield: 8 servings.

PALE GREEN MERINGUE HEARTS WITH PASTEL SHERBETS

4 egg whites
1½ teaspoons vinegar
¼ teaspoon cream of tartar
⅛ teaspoon salt
1¼ cups sugar
Green food coloring
Assorted sherbets

Combine egg whites (at room temperature), vinegar, cream of tartar, and salt in a large mixing bowl; beat until foamy. Gradually add sugar, 1 tablespoon at a time, beating until stiff peaks form. Tint meringue to desired pastel shade of green.

Spoon meringue by ½ cupfuls onto greased, unglazed brown paper. Use back of a spoon to shape meringue into 4-inch hearts. Shape each heart into a shell (sides should be about 1 inch high). Bake at 250° for 1 hour. Cool away from drafts. Spoon sherbet into heart shells and serve immediately. Yield: 8 servings.

WEDDING BREAKFAST AT THE HERMITAGE

The stately Hermitage, built by Andrew Jackson for his wife, Rachel, was the scene of many wedding breakfasts. The open-handed hospitality there was known nationwide, and around Nashville, the Jacksons' friends knew they were welcome to honeymoon at the Hermitage and made free to do so. In fact the front guest room there has been nicknamed "The Bride's Room." One can only imagine the lavishness of the wedding breakfasts Rachel and her staff placed before the honeymooners. A Hermitage wedding breakfast could have been very much like this one.

FRIED COUNTRY SAUSAGE PATTIES
TENNESSEE TURKEY HASH
RICED EGGS
GRITS SOUFFLÉ
APPLES SPECIAL
HOT BISCUITS
TEA MUFFINS

Serves 8

TENNESSEE TURKEY HASH

1 (12- to 13-pound) turkey
4 stalks celery, halved
2 medium onions, quartered
1 bay leaf
1 teaspoon salt
½ teaspoon dried, crushed red pepper
2 quarts water
¼ cup plus 2 tablespoons butter or margarine
½ cup all-purpose flour
3 tablespoons Worcestershire sauce (optional)
½ teaspoon salt
¼ teaspoon white pepper
Fresh parsley sprigs
Pimiento strips

The Hermitage, Andrew Jackson's historic mansion in Nashville.

Photographer: Jim Bathie

Remove giblets and neck from turkey; set aside. Rinse turkey thoroughly with cold water. Place turkey, breast side up, in a deep roasting pan. Insert meat thermometer in breast or meaty part of thigh, making sure it does not touch bone. Place giblets and neck, celery, onion, bay leaf, 1 teaspoon salt, and red pepper around turkey; add 2 quarts water.

Cover and bake at 325° for 3 hours or until meat thermometer registers 185°, basting occasionally with pan drippings.

Remove turkey from cooking liquid; set aside to cool. Remove turkey from bones; cut into bite-size pieces. Cover and refrigerate overnight.

Strain cooking liquid, reserving broth; discard vegetables. Cool broth to room temperature; cover and refrigerate overnight. Lift fat from top of broth; discard fat.

Melt butter in a large Dutch oven over low heat; add flour, and stir until smooth. Cook 1 minute, stirring constantly. Gradually add 6 cups turkey broth; cook over medium heat, stirring constantly, until thickened and bubbly. Stir in Worcestershire sauce, if desired, ½ teaspoon salt, white pepper, and turkey. Cook over low heat, stirring occasionally, until thoroughly heated. Spoon hash into a shallow serving dish. Garnish with parsley sprigs and pimiento strips. Serve hash over hot biscuits or waffles. Yield: 8 servings.

RICED EGGS

3 tablespoons butter or margarine
3 tablespoons all-purpose flour
2 cups milk
1 tablespoon Worcestershire sauce
½ teaspoon salt
Dash of red pepper
8 hard-cooked eggs
1 cup soft breadcrumbs
2 tablespoons butter or margarine, melted

Melt 3 tablespoons butter in a heavy saucepan over low heat; add flour, stirring until smooth. Cook 1 minute, stirring constantly. Gradually add milk and Worcestershire sauce; cook over medium heat, stirring constantly, until mixture is thickened and bubbly. Add salt and pepper; stir well.

Process eggs through a food mill. Stir eggs into sauce. Spoon egg mixture into a lightly greased 1-quart casserole.

Combine breadcrumbs and butter, tossing well. Sprinkle over egg mixture. Bake at 350° for 30 minutes or until bubbly. Serve hot. Yield: 8 servings.

GRITS SOUFFLÉ

1 cup regular grits, uncooked
4 cups boiling water
1 tablespoon salt
½ cup butter or margarine, divided
½ cup milk
3 eggs, separated
½ teaspoon white pepper
¼ teaspoon paprika
½ cup (2 ounces) shredded sharp Cheddar cheese
Additional paprika

Combine grits, water, salt, and 1 tablespoon butter in a medium saucepan. Cook over medium-high heat 5 minutes. Reduce heat; cover and simmer 10 minutes. Add remaining butter, milk, egg yolks, pepper, paprika, and cheese; stir until cheese melts.

Beat egg whites (at room temperature) until stiff peaks form. Gently fold into grits mixture. Spoon into a greased 2-quart soufflé dish; sprinkle heavily with additional paprika. Bake at 350° for 45 minutes. Serve immediately. Yield: 8 servings.

APPLES SPECIAL

1 lemon
1 large orange
4 cups sugar
4 cups water
2 teaspoons ground cinnamon
8 medium-size cooking apples, peeled, cored, and cut into 1-inch wedges

Remove rind from lemon and orange; reserve lemon and orange juice, discarding pulp. Cut lemon and orange rind into thin strips; set aside.

Combine sugar, water, cinnamon, and lemon and orange rind strips in a large Dutch oven. Bring to a boil; reduce heat, and simmer 30 minutes.

Add reserved lemon and orange juice and apples; continue to cook 30 minutes or until apples are golden. Serve hot or cold. Yield: 8 servings.

HOT BISCUITS

2 cups all-purpose flour
1 tablespoon plus 1 teaspoon baking powder
½ teaspoon salt
½ cup shortening
⅔ cup milk

Sift together flour, baking powder, and salt. Cut in shortening with a pastry blender until mixture resembles coarse meal. Sprinkle milk evenly over flour mixture, stirring until dry ingredients are moistened.

Turn dough out onto a well-floured surface; knead lightly 10 to 12 times.

Roll dough to ½-inch thickness; cut with a 2-inch biscuit cutter. Place biscuits on an ungreased baking sheet. Bake at 450° for 8 minutes or until lightly browned. Serve hot. Yield: 1½ dozen.

TEA MUFFINS

½ cup butter or margarine, softened
1 cup sugar
2 eggs, separated
1½ cups all-purpose flour
1½ teaspoons baking powder
½ cup milk
½ teaspoon vanilla extract
Powdered sugar

Cream butter in a medium mixing bowl; gradually add sugar, beating well. Add egg yolks; beat well.

Combine flour and baking powder; add to creamed mixture alternately with milk, beginning and ending with flour mixture. Stir in vanilla.

Beat egg whites (at room temperature) until stiff peaks form. Gently fold into batter. Spoon 1 teaspoon batter into each greased miniature muffin pan. Bake at 350° for 12 minutes or until lightly browned. Cool in pans 10 minutes; remove to wire racks, and cool completely. Sift powdered sugar over tops of muffins. Yield: about 3½ dozen.

The Wedding Breakfast menu in The Hermitage dining room.

WEDDING RECEPTION AT HOME

The home wedding reception is very "Southern." In retrospect, wedding customs on the frontier and in the eastern South were with few exceptions strikingly different in the mid-1800s. Home weddings were the norm in each case, but frontier families, starved for entertainment, considered a wedding to be a public diversion. The groom's attendants gathered at his home before the wedding and, leaving in time to arrive at the bride's house for the noon ceremony, they "ran for the bottle," the winner receiving a bottle of liquor. There was a substantial dinner followed by dancing until dawn. Heavy consumption of liquor was another common denominator: A wealthy Florida woman's diary gave equal space to her sister's satin gown, music, and feasting, and to the champagne drinking that made some grow "lightheaded."

CHEESE BELLS
SOUR CREAM SPINACH DIP
ASSORTED CHEESES AND MEATS
PARTY POPPY SEED ROLLS
MINT TWISTS
BRIDE'S CAKE * GROOM'S CAKE
MONOGRAMMED COOKIES
WEDDING PUNCH
CHAMPAGNE PUNCH

Serves 24

CHEESE BELLS

1 (8-ounce) package cream cheese, softened
2 cups (8 ounces) shredded sharp Cheddar cheese
1 tablespoon grated onion
1 teaspoon Worcestershire sauce
Dash of garlic powder
Dash of hot sauce
½ cup chopped pecans
3 tablespoons minced fresh parsley
Assorted crackers

Combine cheese in a medium mixing bowl; beat at medium speed of an electric mixer until smooth. Stir in onion, Worcestershire sauce, garlic powder, and hot sauce; mix well.

Divide mixture in half; shape each half into a bell. Combine pecans and parsley; roll bells in pecan mixture, and chill several hours. Transfer to a serving platter; serve with crackers. Yield: 24 appetizer servings.

SOUR CREAM SPINACH DIP

1 (16-ounce) carton commercial sour cream
1 cup finely chopped fresh spinach, cleaned (about ¾ pound)
½ cup freeze-dried chives
2 tablespoons minced fresh parsley
1 teaspoon salt
⅛ teaspoon pepper
⅛ teaspoon garlic powder

Combine all ingredients in a medium mixing bowl; mix well. Cover and chill. Serve with assorted raw vegetables. Yield: about 2⅔ cups.

PARTY POPPY SEED ROLLS

4 to 4½ cups all-purpose flour, divided
2 packages dry yeast
2 teaspoons salt
1½ cups milk
¼ cup sugar
¼ cup shortening
2 tablespoons butter or margarine, melted
1 teaspoon poppy seeds

Combine 1½ cups flour, yeast, and salt in a large mixing bowl; stir well. Set aside.

Heat milk, sugar, and shortening in a small saucepan to 120° to 130°. Gradually add to flour mixture, beating well. Stir in enough remaining flour to make a stiff dough.

Turn dough out onto a floured surface, and knead 5 minutes or until dough is smooth and elastic. Place dough in a well-greased bowl, turning to grease top. Cover and let rise in a warm place (85°), free from drafts, 1 hour or until doubled in bulk.

Punch dough down; divide into 24 equal portions. Roll each portion into a ball, and place on buttered baking sheets; press down lightly with fingertips to resemble a bun. Brush rolls with melted butter, and sprinkle with poppy seeds. Cover and repeat rising procedure 30 minutes or until doubled in bulk.

Bake at 400° for 15 minutes or until golden brown. Remove from baking sheets immediately. Cool completely. Split and use as party sandwich buns. Yield: 2 dozen.

MINT TWISTS

2 cups sugar
1 cup water
¼ cup butter or margarine
⅛ teaspoon oil of peppermint
4 drops red food coloring

Combine sugar and water in a large saucepan; bring to a boil, and add butter. Cover and cook over high heat 5 minutes. Uncover and continue cooking until mixture reaches hard ball stage (260°). Remove from heat, and immediately pour syrup onto a buttered marble slab.

Sprinkle oil of peppermint and food coloring over surface of hot syrup; let rest 5 minutes. Begin scraping syrup with metal spatulas into a central mass. Continue scraping and folding until coloring is evenly distributed throughout syrup.

Pull mixture with fingertips, allowing a spread of about 18 inches between hands; fold mixture in half. Repeat this motion rhythmically until consistency of mixture changes from sticky to elastic and glistening.

Begin twisting while folding and pulling. Continue pulling until ridges on the twists begin to hold their shape. This takes 5 to 20 minutes, depending on the weather and your skill.

Shape mint mixture into a 1-inch-thick rope. Using kitchen shears, cut the rope into 1½-inch segments. Twist, pull, and form each segment into desired shapes. Place mints on a wire rack to cool, and cover with a linen towel. Let mints sit overnight or until they become creamy. Wrap mints individually in aluminum foil or place in a sealed container to prevent drying. Yield: about 4 dozen.

BRIDE'S CAKE

1½ cups unsalted butter,
  softened
3 cups sugar, divided
6 cups sifted cake flour
3 tablespoons baking powder
2¼ cups milk
2 teaspoons vanilla extract
10 egg whites
1½ teaspoons salt
Almond-Coconut Filling
Buttercream Frosting
½ pound white chocolate
  (optional)
Green and orange paste food
  coloring

Cream butter in a large mixing bowl; gradually add 2½ cups sugar, beating until light and fluffy.

Sift together flour and baking powder; repeat sifting procedure. Add to creamed mixture alternately with milk, beginning and ending with flour mixture. Stir in vanilla.

Combine egg whites (at room temperature) and salt; beat until foamy. Gradually add remaining sugar, 1 tablespoon at a time, beating until stiff peaks form; fold into batter.

Pour batter into one 4-inch, one 7-inch, and one 10-inch waxed paper-lined and greased round cakepans.

Bake layers at 350° as follows: 10-inch layer for 1 hour; 7-inch layer for 50 minutes; 4-inch layer for 30 minutes. Cake layers will be done when a wooden pick inserted in center comes out clean. Cool in pans 10 minutes; remove from pans, and cool completely on wire racks. Split layers in half horizontally. Spread Almond-Coconut Filling on split layers; cover with tops to reassemble.

Assemble filled layers by placing 10-inch layer on cake plate, and consecutively centering 7-inch and 4-inch layers on top, spreading Buttercream Frosting between each filled layer to secure. Spread top and sides with Buttercream Frosting. Set remaining frosting aside.

If a white chocolate basket and white chocolate leaves are desired to decorate top of cake, melt white chocolate in top of a double boiler over hot, not boiling, water until almost melted. Remove top part of double boiler from water, being careful not to get any water into chocolate. Stir chocolate until melted.

Spoon melted chocolate into basket-shaped candy mold. Allow chocolate to harden in refrigerator; invert mold and tap it gently to release chocolate. Place basket on top of cake.

Using a small artist's brush, "paint" chocolate onto surface of small ivy leaves. Place painted leaves on a waxed paper-lined baking sheet, and chill until hardened. Carefully peel leaves away, and discard. Gently arrange "chocolate leaves" attractively around sides of cake.

Using paste food coloring, tint reserved Buttercream Frosting to desired pastel shades of green and orange. Fill pastry bags with tinted frosting, and attractively pipe clusters of grapes and grapevines onto sides and over top of cake. Yield: one 3-layer tiered cake.

Almond-Coconut Filling:

½ cup sugar
½ cup evaporated milk
2 egg yolks
¼ cup butter or margarine
¼ teaspoon vanilla extract
¼ teaspoon almond extract
½ cup flaked coconut
½ cup finely chopped
  almonds

Combine first 4 ingredients in a medium saucepan; cook over medium heat, stirring constantly, 12 minutes or until mixture thickens. Add remaining ingredients; beat until filling is thick enough to spread. Allow mixture to cool to room temperature. Yield: 1½ cups.

Buttercream Frosting:

1 cup butter or margarine,
  softened
1 cup shortening
1 teaspoon vanilla extract
1 teaspoon almond extract
¼ teaspoon salt
8 cups sifted powdered sugar
¼ cup plus 2 tablespoons
  whipping cream

Combine butter and shortening in a large mixing bowl; beat well with an electric mixer. Add flavorings and salt. Gradually add sugar, 1 cup at a time. Add whipping cream to creamed mixture, beating until smooth enough to spread. Yield: frosting for one 3-layer tiered cake.

delicate, feminine Bride's Cake for an at-home wedding reception.

GROOM'S CAKE

½ cup golden raisins
½ cup raisins
½ cup sherry
1 cup butter, softened
1 cup sugar
4 egg yolks, well beaten
1¼ cups candied red cherries, finely chopped
1¼ cups chopped candied pineapple
1½ cups chopped almonds
2 cups all-purpose flour
¼ teaspoon baking soda
8 egg whites
¼ teaspoon salt
2 (10-ounce) jars apricot preserves
Sifted powdered sugar
Fresh rosemary sprig (optional)

Combine raisins and sherry; set aside.

Cream butter in a large mixing bowl; gradually add 1 cup sugar, beating until light and fluffy. Add egg yolks, beating well. Stir in chopped cherries, pineapple, almonds, and raisin-sherry mixture.

Combine flour and soda, and set aside.

Beat egg whites (at room temperature) in a large mixing bowl until foamy; add salt, beating until stiff peaks form. Gently fold egg whites into batter alternately with flour mixture, beginning and ending with flour mixture.

Spoon batter into 3 waxed paper-lined and greased 9-inch round cakepans. Place a large pan of boiling water on lower oven rack. Bake cake at 275° for 1 hour or until a wooden pick inserted in center comes out clean. Cool in pans 10 minutes; remove layers from pans, and let cool completely.

Spoon apricot preserves into a small saucepan; cook over low heat, stirring frequently, until preserves melt.

Spread preserves between layers and on top and sides of cake. Sprinkle top with powdered sugar. Garnish top of cake with a sprig of fresh rosemary, if desired. Yield: one 3-layer cake.

MONOGRAMMED COOKIES

1½ cups unsalted butter
1½ cups sugar
3 eggs
2 teaspoons vanilla extract
1 teaspoon almond extract
4½ cups all-purpose flour
2 teaspoons salt
2 teaspoons baking powder
Icing (recipe follows)

Cream butter in a large mixing bowl; gradually add sugar, beating until light and fluffy. Add eggs, one at a time, beating well after each addition. Add flavorings, beating well.

Combine flour, salt, and baking powder; gradually add to creamed mixture, mixing well after each addition. Divide dough into 4 equal portions. Cover and chill dough 1 hour.

Roll one portion of dough to ⅛-inch thickness on a lightly floured surface. Cut dough into rounds with a 2½-inch cookie cutter. Place cookies on ungreased baking sheets. Bake at 400° for 6 minutes or until edges are lightly browned. Cool on a wire rack. Repeat procedure with remaining dough.

Spoon icing into a pastry bag with a round tip. Monogram each cookie with bride's and groom's initials. Yield: 5 dozen.

Note: Monogrammed cookies may be frozen in single layers on baking sheets and thawed when ready to use.

Icing:

¾ cup shortening
¼ cup unsalted butter
1 tablespoon whipping cream
1 teaspoon vanilla extract
3 cups sifted powdered sugar

Combine shortening and butter in a medium mixing bowl; beat until well blended. Add whipping cream and vanilla, beating well. Gradually add powdered sugar; beat well after each addition. Yield: icing for 5 dozen cookies.

WEDDING PUNCH

1 (46-ounce) can unsweetened pineapple juice
1 (6-ounce) bottle red maraschino cherries, undrained and chopped
3 (28-ounce) bottles ginger ale, chilled
1 (28-ounce) bottle club soda, chilled
1 quart raspberry sherbet
1 quart lime sherbet

Combine pineapple juice and maraschino cherries, mixing well; chill. To serve, combine chilled mixture, ginger ale, and club soda in a punch bowl. Drop sherbet by scoopfuls into punch. Yield: about 3 quarts.

CHAMPAGNE PUNCH

Whole strawberries
Fresh mint leaves
½ cup light corn syrup
½ cup brandy
1 (750 ml) bottle Sauterne, chilled
1 (28-ounce) bottle club soda, chilled
1 (750 ml) bottle champagne, chilled

Pour water into a 9-cup ring mold to a depth of ¼-inch; freeze until firm. Arrange strawberries and mint leaves on top of frozen layer. Pour ¾ cup ice cold water over top, and freeze. Continue adding ¾ cup ice cold water and freezing after each addition until mold is filled. Freeze overnight until solid.

Combine syrup and brandy in a large punch bowl, stirring until well blended. Stir in Sauterne. Just before serving, stir in club soda and champagne. Remove ice ring from mold, and add to punch bowl. Yield: about 3 quarts.

JUST FAMILY

"Why don't you all come on over for dinner?" "Well, only if you promise not to go to any trouble." "Of course I won't; it's only family!" If this little colloquy sounds familiar, you must be from the South. This attitude of sharing family meals on the spur of the moment is rooted in colonial days when homes were far apart and inns all but non-existent. Every homemaker was prepared to set out extra plates for drop-ins, even strangers.

In Marion Harland's little "Call it luncheon" story, the distraught woman unhinged by unexpected guests was a victim of neglect by town tradesmen; it could hardly have happened to a farm woman. More than one rural home in the nineteenth century regularly set out half a dozen plates more than the family would use. There are true stories about the post-Civil War years when home owners who had plenty of food stationed servants at the roadside to bring in travelers to be fed.

The weekly family gathering, to a Southerner, used to mean "chicken every Sunday." But that chicken could speak with many accents, thanks to the familiar, ongoing flavors that keep our ethnic traditions vibrantly alive. Jewish families take their Friday evening meal together regularly, and it is a truism that nobody makes roast chicken like mother's. It is the "just for family" meals upon which grown-up children look back with fondness; that is where we get the customs we impart to our own children. No matter how many sat down to table, each expected to find his favorite vegetable or dessert, and usually did. Despite all the effort, though, most mothers can recall an instance when a visitor chanced to be present, and she really would make an effort to embellish the food already on the bill of fare: The salad in the "good" crystal bowl, for instance, or the mashed potatoes formed into a ring with the peas inside. Then would come a child's stage whisper, "Why don't we eat like this all the time?"

The moral to the mystique of the Southern family dinner, and being invited to partake of same, is this: Never say "No." Because, if your acquaintance is sufficiently wide, you could be dining informally upon chicken and dumplings, tortillas, veal scallopini, or boliche.

MENU OF MENUS

SUNDAY DINNER AT GRANDMOTHER'S

SUNDAY DINNER AT THE PUREFOY HOTEL

JEWISH SABBATH DINNER

LA COMIDA MEXICANA

SPECIAL ITALIAN FARE

A LATIN FAMILY DINNER

The H.D. Wilson family posed for Charles Franck, New Orleans, c.1890.

SUNDAY DINNER AT GRANDMOTHER'S

The custom of Sunday dinner at Grandmother's was probably responsible for much of the cohesiveness of Southern families, an attribute sometimes mistaken for clannishness. Today's grandmother remembers her grandmother's spacious kitchen, divided into summer kitchen (with gas stove for canning) and winter kitchen (with wood stove for heating and cooking). Sunday dinner started on Saturday with the dressing of chickens and the baking of several desserts. Before church, the table was set, though it was not known how many would turn up.

CHICKEN AND DUMPLINGS
SCALLOPED TOMATOES * BUTTER BEANS
STUFFED CELERY
SALLY LUNN * BUTTERMILK CORNBREAD
GRAM'S TEA CAKES
EASY BLACKBERRY COBBLER
PINEAPPLE CAKE

Serves 8

CHICKEN AND DUMPLINGS

1½ cups all-purpose flour
1 teaspoon salt
¼ teaspoon baking soda
Pinch of sugar
¼ cup shortening
½ cup buttermilk
1 egg, beaten
2 (3- to 4-pound)
    broiler-fryers, cut up
3 cups chicken broth
3 cups water
¾ teaspoon pepper
1 cup milk

Combine flour, salt, soda, and sugar; stir well. Cut in shortening with a pastry blender until mixture resembles coarse meal. Stir in buttermilk and egg. Shape mixture into a ball; cover and place in freezer for 30 to 40 minutes.

Combine chicken, broth, water, and pepper in a large stock pot. Bring to a boil. Reduce heat; cover and simmer 35 minutes or until chicken is tender. Remove chicken from broth; cool. Bone and skin chicken; cut meat into bite-size pieces, and set aside. Strain broth, and return to stock pot.

Turn dumpling dough out onto a heavily floured surface. Roll dough to ⅛-inch thickness; cut into 1-inch squares. Bring chicken broth to a boil. Drop dumpling squares into broth. Add chicken pieces. Reduce heat; cover and simmer 20 minutes. (Do not remove lid or dumplings will be tough.) Stir in milk. Serve immediately. Yield: 8 servings.

SCALLOPED TOMATOES

6 medium-size firm, ripe
    tomatoes, peeled and cut
    into ¼-inch slices
¼ cup finely chopped onion
3 tablespoons chopped green
    pepper
¾ teaspoon sugar
¾ teaspoon salt
¼ teaspoon pepper
3 cups soft breadcrumbs
3 tablespoons butter or
    margarine
½ cup (2 ounces) shredded
    sharp Cheddar cheese

Arrange a layer of tomato slices in bottom of a lightly greased 2-quart casserole. Combine onion and green pepper. Spoon half of mixture over tomato slices. Combine sugar, salt, and pepper; sprinkle half of mixture over vegetables. Place a layer of breadcrumbs over mixture. Repeat layers, ending with breadcrumbs on top. Dot top of casserole with butter.

Bake at 375° for 25 minutes. Sprinkle cheese over top; continue baking an additional 5 minutes. Yield: 8 servings.

BUTTER BEANS

2 (16-ounce) packages frozen
    butter beans
1 teaspoon salt
1 tablespoon butter or
    margarine
⅓ cup whipping cream

Combine butter beans, salt, and water to cover in a large saucepan. Bring to a boil. Reduce heat; cover and simmer 30 minutes or until beans are tender. Drain.

Add butter and whipping cream to beans in saucepan. Cook over low heat, stirring occasionally, 5 minutes or until mixture is thoroughly heated. Yield: 8 servings.

STUFFED CELERY

1 (8-ounce) package cream
    cheese, softened
1 tablespoon plus 1 teaspoon
    whipping cream
½ teaspoon salt
Red pepper to taste
1 bunch celery, washed,
    separated into stalks, and
    cut into 4-inch pieces
⅓ cup finely chopped pecans

Combine first 4 ingredients in a small bowl; beat well. Stuff celery with cream cheese mixture; roll in pecans. Chill. Yield: about 1½ dozen.

Motto embroidered from a punched paper pattern, c.1870.

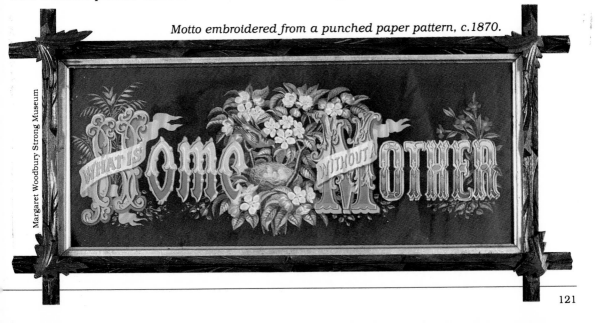

Margaret Woodbury Strong Museum

SALLY LUNN

1 package dry yeast
¼ cup warm water (105°
   to 115°)
2 tablespoons butter or
   margarine, softened
½ cup sugar
2 eggs
1 teaspoon salt
3½ cups all-purpose flour,
   divided
1 cup warm milk (105° to
   115°)

Dissolve yeast in warm water, stirring well. Let stand 5 minutes or until bubbly.

Cream butter in a medium mixing bowl; gradually add sugar, beating well. Add eggs and salt, beating until smooth.

Add 1½ cups flour to creamed mixture; beat well. Stir in milk and dissolved yeast, mixing well. Gradually stir in remaining flour to make a soft dough.

Cover and let rise in a warm place (85°), free from drafts, 1 hour or until doubled in bulk. Stir dough down; spoon batter into a well-greased 10-inch Bundt pan. Cover and repeat rising procedure 30 minutes or until doubled in bulk.

Bake at 325° for 10 minutes. Increase temperature to 375°; bake 20 minutes or until golden brown. Cool in pan 10 minutes. Remove from pan, and place on wire rack to cool. Yield: one 10-inch loaf.

Turn-of-the-century trade card for Fleischmann's Yeast.

Collection of Business Americana

BUTTERMILK CORNBREAD

1 cup cornmeal
1 cup all-purpose flour
2 teaspoons baking powder
1 teaspoon salt
1 teaspoon baking soda
2 cups buttermilk
2 eggs, beaten
2 tablespoons bacon
   drippings or shortening,
   melted

Combine cornmeal, flour, baking powder, and salt; mix well. Dissolve soda in buttermilk. Add buttermilk mixture, eggs, and bacon drippings to dry ingredients; stir just until moistened.

Pour batter into a greased 9-inch cast-iron skillet. Bake at 450° for 20 minutes or until browned. Cut into wedges, and serve hot. Yield: 8 servings.

GRAM'S TEA CAKES

½ cup butter or margarine,
   softened
1 cup sugar
2 eggs, beaten
1 teaspoon vanilla extract
⅓ cup milk
3 cups all-purpose flour,
   divided
2 teaspoons baking powder
½ teaspoon ground nutmeg

Cream butter in a large mixing bowl; gradually add sugar, beating well. Add eggs, vanilla, and milk; beat well.

Combine 1 cup flour, baking powder, and nutmeg. Add to creamed mixture, mixing well. Gradually add remaining flour. Divide dough in half; wrap in waxed paper, and chill at least 30 minutes.

Roll half of dough to ¼-inch thickness on a floured surface. Cut dough with a 2½-inch biscuit cutter. Place on a lightly greased baking sheet. Bake at 350° for 12 minutes or until edges are lightly browned. Cool cookies on a wire rack. Repeat rolling, cutting, and baking procedure with remaining dough. Yield: 2 dozen.

Raphaelle Peale's painting of a bowl of blackberries and perfect leaves, 1813.

EASY BLACKBERRY COBBLER

½ cup butter or margarine
1 cup all-purpose flour
1 cup sugar
1 tablespoon baking powder
⅛ teaspoon salt
⅔ cup milk
1 (16-ounce) package frozen
  blackberries, thawed
Vanilla ice cream (optional)

Melt butter in a 2-quart casserole. Combine flour, sugar, baking powder, salt, and milk in a small mixing bowl; mix well. Pour mixture over melted butter; do not stir. Spoon blackberries over batter; do not stir. Bake at 350° for 45 minutes or until golden brown. Cobbler may be served hot or cold with ice cream, if desired. Yield: 8 servings.

PINEAPPLE CAKE

½ cup shortening
1½ cups sugar
2 eggs
2 cups all-purpose flour
2 teaspoons baking powder
¼ teaspoon baking soda
1 cup buttermilk
1 teaspoon vanilla extract
Pineapple Frosting

Cream shortening in a medium mixing bowl; gradually add sugar, beating well. Add eggs, one at a time, beating well after each addition.

Combine flour, baking powder, and soda. Add flour mixture to creamed mixture alternately with buttermilk, beginning and ending with flour mixture. Stir in vanilla.

Pour batter into 2 greased and floured 8-inch round cakepans.

Bake at 350° for 35 minutes or until a wooden pick inserted in center comes out clean. Cool in pans 10 minutes; remove layers from pans, and cool completely.

Spread Pineapple Frosting between layers and on top of cake. Yield: one 2-layer cake.

Pineapple Frosting:

1 cup evaporated milk
1 cup sugar
3 egg yolks
½ cup butter or margarine
1 teaspoon vanilla extract
1 (20-ounce) can crushed
  pineapple, drained

Combine first 4 ingredients in a heavy saucepan. Cook over medium heat, stirring constantly, until mixture thickens. Stir in vanilla and pineapple; mix well. Cool completely. Yield: frosting for one 2-layer cake.

123

SUNDAY DINNER AT THE PUREFOY HOTEL

The Purefoy Hotel in Talladega, Alabama, lives in the memory of everyone who ate there between 1920 and 1961, when it closed permanently. For a special occasion, a family would drive half a day to join the crowd at the nationally famous 88-room hotel for Sunday dinner, the menu for which ran to some forty items. Eva Brunson Purefoy personally supervised all food preparation and kept going back to the business for the love of it. There probably isn't a restaurant in the country offering so extensive a family-style menu today, but the idea of closing down the kitchen and taking the family out to Sunday dinner is still a good one. Just imagine this menu multiplied by four for a Sunday dinner at the Purefoy!

OLD-FASHIONED CHEESE STRAWS
POT ROAST
or
ROAST CHICKEN
ASPARAGUS CASSEROLE
CREAMED GREEN PEAS
BAKED WILD RICE
PEAR SALAD
STUFFED PRUNES
BRAN MUFFINS
DATE PUDDING * APRICOT SHERBET

Serves 8

Birmingham Public Library

To dine at the Purefoy Hotel in 1946 was to partake of a banquet of multiple selections costing only $1.65 for all you could eat!

OLD-FASHIONED CHEESE STRAWS

4 cups (16 ounces) shredded extra sharp Cheddar cheese
½ cup butter or margarine, softened
2 cups all-purpose flour
2 teaspoons baking powder
1 teaspoon salt
½ teaspoon paprika
⅛ to ¼ teaspoon red pepper
Additional paprika

Combine cheese and butter; mix well. Set aside.

Combine flour, baking powder, salt, ½ teaspoon paprika, and pepper in a large mixing bowl, mixing well. Gradually add flour mixture to cheese mixture, mixing until dough is no longer crumbly. Form dough into a ball.

Use a cookie gun to shape dough into straws, following manufacturer's instructions, or use the following procedure: Divide dough into fourths; roll each portion into a rectangle ⅓-inch thick on waxed paper. Use a pastry wheel to cut dough into 4- x ½-inch strips.

Place strips or straws on ungreased baking sheets. Bake at 450° for 10 minutes or until lightly browned. Sprinkle with additional paprika. Store straws in airtight containers, placing waxed paper between layers. Yield: about 4 dozen.

Exterior of the Purefoy Hotel, Talladega, Alabama, showing the verandas where patrons were wont to doze after one of Mrs. Purefoy's Sunday dinners.

Cooper-Hewitt Museum

POT ROAST

1 (4-pound) boneless chuck roast
⅛ pound salt pork, thinly sliced
⅛ teaspoon pepper
1 clove garlic, minced
1 teaspoon salt
2 tablespoons all-purpose flour
¼ cup shortening
2 medium onions, sliced
1 bay leaf
1 cup water

Cut deep slits randomly in roast. Rub salt pork slices with pepper, and insert slices into slits. Rub entire surface of roast with garlic, salt, and flour.

Brown roast on all sides in hot shortening in a large Dutch oven. Add sliced onion, bay leaf, and 1 cup water. Cover and simmer 2½ hours or until meat is tender.

Transfer roast to a serving platter. Remove bay leaf from gravy and discard. (Gravy may be thickened with additional flour, if desired). Serve gravy with roast. Yield: 8 servings.

Bran Muffins surrounded by Pear Salad, Old-Fashioned Cheese Straws, and Stuffed Prunes.

ROAST CHICKEN

2 (3- to 3½-pound)
  broiler-fryers, cut up
¼ cup plus 2 tablespoons
  shortening
2 teaspoons salt
½ teaspoon pepper
2 cups water
¼ cup butter or margarine,
  melted
¼ cup all-purpose flour
2 (2½-ounce) jars sliced
  mushrooms, drained

Brown chicken in shortening over low heat; transfer to a covered roasting pan. Sprinkle chicken with salt and pepper. Add water; cover and bake at 350° for 50 minutes or until chicken is tender. Remove chicken to a heated serving platter; reserving pan liquid.

Combine melted butter and flour, stirring until a smooth paste is formed. Heat reserved pan liquid in a small saucepan over medium heat. Add flour mixture, stirring until well blended. Cook over medium heat 1 minute, stirring constantly. Add mushrooms; stir well. Pour sauce over chicken; serve hot. Yield: 8 servings.

ASPARAGUS CASSEROLE

¼ cup butter or margarine
¼ cup all-purpose flour
2 cups milk
¾ teaspoon salt
Dash of white pepper
2 (15-ounce) cans asparagus
  spears, drained
3 tablespoons fine, dry
  breadcrumbs
1½ cups (6 ounces) shredded
  sharp Cheddar cheese

Melt butter in a heavy saucepan over low heat; add flour, stirring until smooth. Cook 1 minute, stirring constantly. Gradually add milk; cook over medium heat, stirring constantly, until thickened and bubbly. Add salt and pepper, mixing well.

Layer half each of asparagus spears, white sauce, breadcrumbs, and cheese in a lightly greased 10- x 6- x 2-inch baking dish. Repeat layers, reserving cheese. Set cheese aside.

Bake at 350° for 20 minutes; sprinkle with remaining cheese, and continue baking 5 minutes or until cheese melts. Serve hot. Yield: 8 servings.

CREAMED GREEN PEAS

2 (10-ounce) packages frozen
  green peas
1 cup water
½ teaspoon salt
⅛ teaspoon pepper
1 teaspoon sugar
2 tablespoons all-purpose
  flour
2 tablespoons butter or
  margarine, melted
½ cup milk

Combine peas, water, salt, pepper, and sugar in a medium saucepan. Bring to a boil; reduce heat, and cook over medium heat 8 minutes or until peas are tender.

Combine flour and butter; stir until a smooth paste is formed. Add flour mixture to peas; stir well. Gradually add milk to pea mixture; cook over low heat 5 minutes or until thickened, stirring frequently. Serve immediately. Yield: 8 servings.

BAKED WILD RICE

½ pound fresh mushrooms, sliced
½ cup butter or margarine, divided
1 (8-ounce) package wild rice
¼ cup chopped green onion
3 cups chicken broth
½ cup slivered almonds

Sauté mushrooms in ¼ cup plus 2 tablespoons butter in a large skillet. Remove mushrooms; set aside. Reserve butter in skillet. Add rice to skillet; cook over medium heat, 5 minutes, stirring constantly. Stir in mushrooms, green onion, and broth. Spoon mixture into a lightly greased 2-quart casserole. Cover and bake at 350° for 1 hour. Uncover and bake an additional 15 minutes.

Sauté almonds in remaining butter. Stir into rice mixture, and serve immediately. Yield: 8 servings.

PEAR SALAD

2 (16-ounce) cans pear halves, undrained
2 (3-ounce) packages cream cheese, softened
⅓ cup finely chopped pecans
Red maraschino cherries, quartered
Lettuce leaves

Drain pears, reserving 3 tablespoons syrup. Combine cream cheese and syrup, beating until smooth; spoon 1 tablespoon mixture onto each pear half.

Lightly sprinkle chopped pecans over topping and garnish with maraschino cherries. Serve on lettuce leaves. Yield: 8 servings.

STUFFED PRUNES

12 large pitted prunes
1 (3-ounce) package cream cheese, softened
½ cup finely chopped pecans
Lettuce leaves (optional)

Soak prunes overnight in water to cover.

Place prunes and water in a saucepan; simmer 15 minutes. Remove from heat; drain prunes, reserving 3 tablespoons liquid. Slice prunes three-quarters open. Set aside.

Combine cream cheese, pecans, and reserved liquid; mix well. Stuff each prune with 1½ teaspoons cream cheese mixture. Serve on lettuce leaves, if desired. Yield: 1 dozen.

BRAN MUFFINS

1 cup wheat bran cereal
1 cup all-purpose flour
2 tablespoons sugar
3½ teaspoons baking powder
¼ teaspoon salt
2 eggs, beaten
¾ cup milk
3 tablespoons butter or margarine, melted

Combine first 5 ingredients in a medium mixing bowl, stirring well. Make a well in center of mixture. Add eggs, milk, and butter; stir just until dry ingredients are moistened. Spoon mixture into greased muffin pans, filling two-thirds full. Bake at 450° for 12 minutes. Yield: 1 dozen.

DATE PUDDING

3 cups large marshmallows, cut into eighths
3 cups coarsely crushed graham crackers
2 (6-ounce) jars red maraschino cherries, drained and halved
1 cup pitted dates, chopped
1 cup chopped pecans
3 cups whipping cream
¾ cup sugar

Combine marshmallows, graham crackers, cherries, dates, and pecans in a large mixing bowl. Set aside.

Beat whipping cream until foamy; gradually add sugar, 1 tablespoon at a time, beating until soft peaks form. Fold into fruit mixture. Chill. Spoon into individual compotes or serving dishes. Yield: 8 servings.

APRICOT SHERBET

1 quart water
2 cups sugar
2 envelopes unflavored gelatin
½ cup cold water
1 (17-ounce) can apricot halves, undrained and mashed
1 cup orange juice
¼ cup plus 2 tablespoons lemon juice
2 egg whites

Combine 1 quart water and sugar in a Dutch oven. Bring to a boil; reduce heat, and simmer 20 minutes or until slightly thickened. Soften gelatin in ½ cup cold water. Add softened gelatin to syrup mixture; stir until gelatin completely dissolves. Cool.

Combine gelatin mixture, apricots, orange juice, and lemon juice; stir well.

Beat egg whites (at room temperature) until stiff peaks form. Fold into apricot mixture. Pour into freezer can of a 1-gallon hand-turned or electric freezer. Freeze according to manufacturer's instructions. Let ripen 1 hour before serving. Yield: 3 quarts.

Elaborate three-dimensional Jewish greeting card, c.1910.

JEWISH SABBATH DINNER

Unlike so many Southerners, the Jewish people did not come here from just one place, as did, say, the Moravians or the Czechs. From Germany they came, and from Lithuania, Poland, Prussia, Austria-Hungary. It has been their strength that they have shared a language, Hebrew, and the centuries of cultural and religious tradition. The family's weekly observance of the Sabbath is bound by strict rules. The meals served on Friday evening and after Saturday's service at the synagogue must be prepared on Friday before sundown, which marks the start of the Sabbath. An ideal dish is Cholent, a long-cooking, make-ahead stew invented generations ago.

CHOPPED LIVER MOLD
CHOLENT
CABBAGE ROLLS
SPICY CARROTS
CHALLAH
FRESH FRUIT
CHOCOLATE MANDEL BREAD

Serves 8

CHOPPED LIVER MOLD

1 pound chicken livers
1 large onion, chopped
1 tablespoon vegetable oil
2 eggs, beaten
½ teaspoon salt
⅛ teaspoon pepper
Fresh parsley sprigs
Assorted crackers

Place livers on a rack in broiler pan. Broil 5 to 6 inches from heat, 3 to 5 minutes on each side or just until pink.

Sauté onion in hot oil in a medium skillet until tender; stir in eggs, salt, and pepper. Cook over medium heat, stirring constantly, until eggs are scrambled. Spoon liver and onion mixture into container of an electric blender; process until smooth.

Spoon mixture into a lightly oiled 2½-cup mold. Chill several hours or overnight. Invert mold onto a serving platter; garnish with parsley. Serve with crackers. Yield: 8 appetizer servings.

CHOLENT

1 (3- to 4-pound) beef brisket
2 tablespoons vegetable oil
2 cups dried lima beans
½ cup barley
1 large onion, diced
1 (1-pound) soup bone
8 medium-size baking
  potatoes, peeled
1 tablespoon salt
1 teaspoon pepper
1 teaspoon garlic powder
1 teaspoon paprika
4 cups water

Brown brisket on all sides in hot oil in a large skillet, and set aside.

Place brisket in center of a large roasting pan; add lima beans, barley, onion, soup bone, and potatoes.

Sprinkle with seasonings. Add water. Cover and bake at 250° for 5 hours. Remove roast to a large serving platter; surround with vegetables. Yield: 8 servings.

CABBAGE ROLLS

1 pound ground chuck
2 eggs, beaten
1 small onion, chopped
2¾ tablespoons regular rice,
  uncooked
½ teaspoon salt
¼ teaspoon pepper
¼ teaspoon garlic powder
1 large cabbage
1 medium onion, chopped
½ cup shortening, melted
1 (1-pound) soup bone
1 (14½-ounce) can whole
  tomatoes, undrained and
  chopped
1 (8-ounce) can tomato sauce
1 cup plus 2½ tablespoons
  firmly packed brown sugar
Dash of sour salt

Combine ground chuck, eggs, 1 small chopped onion, rice, salt, pepper, and garlic powder, mixing well. Set aside.

Turn cabbage, core side up. Using a sharp knife, make an incision across the base of the outermost leaf. Gently peel away the leaf. Repeat this process until leaves can no longer be removed without tearing.

Make additional incisions around the base of the next outermost leaves. Place cabbage, stem side up, in a colander. Pour boiling water over cabbage until leaves can be easily removed. Repeat procedure until all leaves have been removed.

Place 1 tablespoon meat mixture in the base of a cabbage leaf. Roll leaf jellyroll fashion until the mid-section is reached. Fold left side of leaf inward, and roll up remaining length of the leaf. Carefully stuff in the open end, using fingertips. Repeat with remaining

meat mixture and cabbage leaves.

Sauté remaining chopped onion in shortening in a large Dutch oven. Add soup bone and tomatoes; stir gently.

Alternate layers of cabbage rolls and tomato sauce over sautéed onion and tomatoes. Do not stir. Add water to cover. Cover and cook over medium heat 30 minutes.

Add brown sugar and sour salt; stir gently. Cover and cook over medium heat 1 hour. Uncover and cook 1 hour.

Remove cabbage rolls from cooking liquid, and place on a warm serving platter. Serve immediately. Yield: 8 servings.

SPICY CARROTS

2 pounds carrots, scraped
4 cups water
3 teaspoons salt, divided
¼ cup butter or margarine
2 small onions, thinly sliced
2 small cloves garlic
2 tablespoons vinegar
2 tablespoons chopped chives

Cut carrots crosswise into ½-inch slices. Combine water and 2 teaspoons salt in a small Dutch oven; bring to a boil. Add carrots; reduce heat, and cook 5 minutes. Drain.

Add butter, onion, garlic, and remaining salt to carrots in Dutch oven. Cover; cook over low heat, stirring occasionally, 10 minutes. Remove garlic; discard. Add vinegar; mix well. Transfer to a serving bowl; sprinkle with chives. Serve hot. Yield: 8 servings.

CHALLAH

1 package dry yeast
⅓ cup sugar, divided
¼ cup warm water (105°
  to 115°)
½ cup margarine,
  softened
½ teaspoon salt
½ cup frozen non-dairy
  creamer, thawed
3 eggs, beaten
1 egg yolk
3¼ cups all-purpose flour,
  divided
1 egg yolk
2 tablespoons water

Dissolve yeast and 1 teaspoon sugar in warm water, stirring well. Let stand 5 minutes or until bubbly.

Cream ½ cup margarine in a large mixing bowl; gradually add remaining sugar and salt, beating well. Scald non-dairy creamer; let cool to 105° to 115°. Add non-dairy creamer, yeast mixture, eggs, and 1 yolk, stirring well. Gradually add 2 cups flour, beating well. Stir in remaining 1¼ cups flour (dough will be sticky).

Place dough in a well-greased bowl, turning to grease top. Cover and let rise in a warm place (85°), free from drafts, 1 hour or until doubled in bulk. Stir dough down. Cover and refrigerate dough for at least 4 hours.

Punch dough down; let rest 5 minutes. Divide dough in half. Divide one half into 3 equal portions; set aside remaining half. Shape each portion into a 10-inch rope. Braid ropes, pinching ends to seal. Place braided loaf in a greased 8-inch loafpan. Repeat procedure with remaining half of dough. Cover and repeat rising procedure 1 hour or until doubled in bulk.

Combine remaining yolk and 2 tablespoons water; beat well. Gently brush over tops of loaves. Bake at 350° for 20 minutes or until loaves sound hollow when tapped. Remove bread from pans immediately, and cool on wire racks. Slice and serve warm. Yield: 2 loaves.

Golden Challah to serve with Cholent on platter at rear.

CHOCOLATE MANDEL BREAD

1 (6-ounce) package
  semisweet chocolate
  morsels
4 eggs, beaten
1½ cups sugar
¾ cup vegetable oil
1 teaspoon vanilla extract
2½ cups all-purpose flour
2 teaspoons baking powder
½ teaspoon salt
1 cup finely chopped almonds

Place chocolate in top of a double boiler; bring water to a boil. Reduce heat to low, and cook, stirring frequently, until chocolate melts. Cool.

Combine eggs, sugar, oil, and vanilla in a large mixing bowl; beat until smooth. Add melted chocolate, mixing well.

Combine flour, baking powder, and salt; add to chocolate mixture, beating well. Stir in almonds. Pour into two greased 8-inch square baking pans. Bake at 350° for 20 minutes. Cool 5 minutes in pan, and cut into 4-x ½-inch bars.

Place bars on ungreased baking sheets. Bake at 275° for 10 minutes; turn bars, and bake 10 minutes or until dry and crusty. Yield: 64 bars.

LA COMIDA MEXICANA

There is a large segment of the Texas population to whom going home for a family dinner means Mexican food. After all, Texas shares more than 300 years of history with Mexico. The few "Anglos" in Texas were concentrated along the San Antonio River and in east Texas until 1824, when Mexico legalized their immigration into the territory. While the Anglo-Americans outnumber the many other ethnic groups in Texas, the Mexican influence is felt in Texas laws, architecture, and, especially, food. Mexican cuisine came out of improvisation by everyday cooks who based their recipes on available ingredients and cooked them with the simplest facilities. The time-honored tortillas, refried beans, beef, and spices all come together in this Mexican home-cooked dinner that may begin with the Mexican favorite, Margaritas.

MARGARITAS
TORTILLA SOUP
CARNE GUISADA ON RICE
REFRIED BLACK BEANS
FLOUR TORTILLAS
MANGO CUSTARD

Serves 6

MARGARITAS

Lime juice
Salt
4½ cups crushed ice
⅓ cup tequila
⅓ cup lime juice
⅓ cup Triple Sec
Lime slices (optional)

Dip rims of cocktail glasses in lime juice; dip in a shallow dish of salt to coat rims of glasses.

Combine crushed ice, tequila, ⅓ cup lime juice, and Triple Sec in container of an electric blender; process until very frothy. Pour into prepared cocktail glasses, and garnish with lime slices, if desired. Yield: about 5 cups.

Note: Sweetened lime juice may be used, if desired.

TORTILLA SOUP

6 corn tortillas, cut into
   ¼-inch strips
3 tablespoons vegetable oil
8 cups chicken broth
2 medium-size firm, ripe
   tomatoes, peeled and
   chopped
8 green onions, chopped
¼ cup grated Parmesan
   cheese

Sauté tortilla strips in oil over low heat; drain and set aside.

Combine chicken broth, tomatoes, onion, and tortilla strips in a large Dutch oven. Bring to a boil; reduce heat, and simmer 20 minutes. Spoon soup into individual serving bowls, and sprinkle with cheese. Yield: 6 servings.

CARNE GUISADA ON RICE

2½ pounds boneless round
   steak, cut into ½-inch cubes
2 tablespoons vegetable oil
1 tablespoon all-purpose flour
1 (10-ounce) can tomatoes
   and green chilies, undrained
   and chopped
1 (8-ounce) can tomato sauce
2 tablespoons chopped green
   pepper
2 tablespoons chopped onion
2 tablespoons chopped
   tomato
2 cloves garlic, minced
½ teaspoon salt
½ teaspoon cumin
⅛ teaspoon pepper
Hot cooked rice
Jalapeño pepper slices
   (optional)

Brown steak on all sides in hot oil in a large skillet. Sprinkle with flour; stir well. Add next 9 ingredients. Bring to a boil; reduce heat, and simmer 45 minutes or until mixture is thickened. Serve stew over hot cooked rice. Garnish with Jalapeño pepper slices, if desired. Yield: 6 servings.

Mexican metate or grinding stone.

Carne Guisada on Rice (front) with Flour Tortillas and Refried Black Beans.

FLOUR TORTILLAS

4 cups all-purpose flour
2 teaspoons salt
⅛ teaspoon baking powder
⅔ cup shortening
1 cup plus 3 tablespoons hot water

Combine dry ingredients; stir well. Cut in shortening with a pastry blender until mixture resembles coarse meal. Gradually stir in water, mixing well.

Shape dough into 1½-inch balls, and place on a lightly floured surface. Roll each ball into a very thin circle about 6 inches in diameter.

Cook tortillas in an ungreased skillet over medium-high heat about 2 minutes on each side or until lightly browned. Pat tortillas lightly with a spatula while browning the second side if they puff during cooking. Serve hot with butter, if desired. Yield: about 2 dozen.

MANGO CUSTARD

4 (9-ounce) cans sliced mangos, undrained
1 (5⅓-ounce) can evaporated milk
⅔ cup sweetened condensed milk
1 tablespoon amaretto

Drain mangos, reserving ½ cup liquid. Combine mangos, reserved juice, milk, and amaretto in a medium mixing bowl. Beat at medium speed of an electric mixer 5 minutes. Spoon mixture into individual serving dishes. Cover and refrigerate several hours before serving. Yield: 6 servings.

REFRIED BLACK BEANS

1 pound dried black beans
5 slices bacon, cut into 3-inch pieces
1 green onion, chopped
1 teaspoon chopped fresh parsley
1 clove garlic, minced
1½ teaspoons salt
1 quart water
2 tablespoons bacon drippings

Sort and wash beans; place in a large Dutch oven. Cover with water 2 inches above beans; let soak overnight. Drain.

Combine beans, bacon, onion, parsley, garlic, salt, and 1 quart water in a large Dutch oven. Bring to a boil. Reduce heat; cover and simmer 45 minutes or until beans are tender. Mash bean mixture.

Melt bacon drippings over low heat in a heavy skillet. Add bean mixture; cook over medium heat 10 minutes or until mixture becomes dry. Serve hot. Yield: 6 servings.

SPECIAL ITALIAN FARE

It has been said that a fine antipasto can be the ruination of the best Italian dinner. That is simply because the elements of antipasto (or "before the meal") are so tempting that one can munch his appetite away before the meal begins. That is one mishap that never befalls the Southerner of Italian ancestry; he knows how to temper his antipasto consumption. It is the tyro who fills himself on bread sticks, marinated mushrooms, and assorted sausages in advance. The stuffed artichokes in this menu are a splendid first course. The pasta, so often seen as a first course, appears here in an unusual soufflé, teaming up with tomatoes and cheese to accompany the scallopini. Dessert is an appropriately light fruit and cheese combination.

ANTIPASTO TRAY
STUFFED ARTICHOKES SICILIAN
VEAL SCALLOPINI
TOMATO VERMICELLI SOUFFLÉ
ITALIAN ROASTED PEPPERS
GORGONZOLA PEARS

Serves 6

STUFFED ARTICHOKES SICILIAN

6 artichokes
1½ cups fine, dry breadcrumbs
1½ tablespoons grated Romano cheese
1 clove garlic, minced
1 teaspoon ground oregano
½ cup vegetable oil
Lemon twists

Wash artichokes by plunging up and down in cold water. Cut off stem end, and trim ½ inch from top of each artichoke. Remove any loose bottom leaves. With scissors, trim away one-fourth of each outer leaf.

Combine breadcrumbs, cheese, garlic, and oregano; mix well. Spread leaves of each artichoke apart, and spoon breadcrumb stuffing onto leaves.

Place stuffed artichokes in a large Dutch oven with about 3 inches of water. Pour vegetable oil evenly over tops of artichokes. Cover and cook over medium heat 1 hour.

Using a slotted spoon, transfer artichokes to a serving platter, and garnish with lemon twists. Yield: 6 servings.

VEAL SCALLOPINI

1½ pounds veal cutlets
¼ cup vegetable oil
1 medium onion, thinly sliced
½ pound fresh mushrooms, sliced
1 clove garlic, minced
2½ tablespoons all-purpose flour
¾ teaspoon salt
¼ teaspoon pepper
½ cup dry white wine
1 cup water
Chopped fresh parsley (optional)

Flatten cutlets to ¼-inch thickness, using a meat mallet or rolling pin. Cut into serving-size pieces. Sauté cutlets in oil in a large skillet until browned; remove from skillet, and set aside. Reserve oil in skillet.

Add onion, mushrooms, and garlic to skillet; sauté until tender. Add flour, salt, and pepper, stirring well. Cook 1 minute, stirring constantly. Add wine, and cook over medium heat until thickened.

Return cutlets to skillet; pour water over cutlets. Cover and cook over low heat 45 minutes or until veal is tender.

Transfer veal to a serving dish; pour mushroom gravy over top. Sprinkle with parsley, if desired. Yield: 6 servings.

Pears stuffed with Gorgonzola, a creamy, strong Italian cheese produced in Lombardy.

TOMATO VERMICELLI SOUFFLE

1 (14½-ounce) can whole
   tomatoes, undrained
3 tablespoons olive oil
2 tablespoons all-purpose
   flour
½ cup grated Romano cheese
Salt and pepper to taste
1 (8-ounce) package
   vermicelli, broken into
   1-inch pieces
3 eggs, separated

Drain and chop tomatoes, reserving ½ cup liquid; set aside.

Heat olive oil in a large skillet; add flour, stirring until smooth. Gradually add reserved tomato liquid; cook over medium heat 2 minutes, stirring constantly. Add reserved tomatoes; continue cooking, stirring constantly, until mixture is thickened and bubbly. Stir in cheese, and salt and pepper; mix well.

Cook vermicelli according to package directions; drain. Combine tomato mixture and vermicelli, mixing well. Beat egg yolks in a medium mixing bowl until thick and lemon colored. Gradually stir one-fourth vermicelli mixture into yolks; add to remaining mixture, stirring well.

Beat egg whites (at room temperature) until stiff but not dry. Fold into vermicelli mixture; spoon into a lightly greased 1½-quart casserole. Bake at 350° for 10 minutes. Serve immediately. Yield: 6 servings.

ITALIAN ROASTED PEPPERS

4 medium-size green peppers
4 medium-size red peppers
¼ cup plus 1 tablespoon
   chopped onion
2 cloves garlic, minced
2½ tablespoons butter or
   margarine
Salt to taste

Place whole peppers on broiler rack. Place rack 6 to 7 inches from heat. Broil 3 minutes on each side or until skin begins to bubble. Remove from oven, and let cool to touch. Rinse peppers with cool water, and remove bubbled skin. Remove and discard seeds. Slice peppers into ¼-inch-wide strips. Set aside.

Sauté onion and garlic in butter until tender; remove from heat, and add pepper strips. Toss gently to coat. Add salt to taste. Serve immediately. Yield: 6 servings.

GORGONZOLA PEARS

6 ripe pears
½ cup lemon juice, divided
3 cups sugar
3 cups water
4 ounces Gorgonzola cheese
½ cup unsalted butter,
   softened

Peel pears; remove core from bottom, leaving stem intact. Slice ¼ inch from bottom of each pear, and brush pears with ¼ cup lemon juice.

Combine sugar, water, and remaining lemon juice in a Dutch oven; bring to a boil. Place pears upright in Dutch oven; spoon syrup over pears. Reduce heat; cover and simmer 15 minutes or until tender. Let pears cool in syrup.

Combine cheese and butter; beat well. Fill pears with cheese mixture; chill. Cut in ½-inch-thick slices to serve. Yield: 6 servings.

LATIN FAMILY DINNER

It was the sixteenth-century Spanish explorers who brought the seeds of Florida's citrus money crop. And there are families and foodways in the state today that are traceable to the same beginnings. Cubans came later and blended their special touch with the Spanish cuisine, resulting in some of the South's most distinctive regional cooking. Black beans and rice, long a mainstay of the Latin diet, combine to make an almost perfect protein. Boliche, the superb eye of beef round, stuffed with a pungent sausage-vegetable mixture, will appear on many a family dinner table as well as the grapefruit-avocado salad that is as close as the back yard. Dessert, to the family of Spanish background, probably means a butter-smooth flan.

SPANISH BOLICHE WITH CARROTS
FLORIDA GRAPEFRUIT-AVOCADO SALAD
BLACK BEANS AND
RICE CASSEROLE
CUBAN BREAD
SPANISH FLAN

Serves 12

SPANISH BOLICHE WITH CARROTS

2 ounces pepperoni slices
10 slices bacon
¼ cup pimiento-stuffed olives
1 (3- to 3½-pound) beef eye of round roast, cut with a pocket
2 tablespoons vegetable oil
1⅔ cups chopped onion
½ cup chopped celery
½ cup chopped green pepper
1 large tomato, peeled, seeded, and chopped
¾ cup Burgundy or other dry red wine
½ teaspoon dried whole oregano
1 bay leaf
1 teaspoon salt
⅛ teaspoon pepper
8 carrots, scraped and cut into 2-inch pieces

Process pepperoni slices, bacon, and olives through the fine cutter of a meat grinder.
Stuff pocket of roast with pepperoni mixture; secure opening with wooden picks. Brown beef on all sides in hot oil in a large Dutch oven. Remove beef to a covered roasting pan, reserving pan drippings in Dutch oven. Sauté onion, celery, and green pepper in reserved pan drippings. Add tomato, wine, oregano, bay leaf, salt, and pepper; simmer 5 minutes. Pour sauce over eye of round. Cover and bake at 300° for 2 hours or until roast is tender.

Remove meat from sauce; cool. Wrap tightly in aluminum foil; refrigerate overnight. Refrigerate sauce and vegetables overnight. Remove fat layer from sauce, and discard. Strain sauce through a sieve; discard vegetables and bay leaf. Place sauce and carrots in a medium saucepan; cook over medium heat 10 minutes or until carrots are tender.

Cut roast into ⅛-inch-thick slices, and arrange on an oven-proof serving platter. Cover with aluminum foil. Bake at 300° for 20 minutes. Arrange carrots around beef, and serve with sauce. Yield: 12 servings.

FLORIDA GRAPEFRUIT-AVOCADO SALAD

3 large grapefruits
3 avocados, peeled, seeded, and sliced
Lettuce leaves
1 (8-ounce) carton commercial sour cream
¾ cup mayonnaise
2 tablespoons tarragon vinegar
¼ cup chopped fresh parsley
¼ cup finely chopped onion
¼ teaspoon garlic salt
⅛ teaspoon red pepper

Peel and section grapefruits; reserve juice that drains from grapefruit. Sprinkle avocado slices with reserved grapefruit juice. Arrange grapefruit sections and avocado slices pinwheel fashion on a lettuce-lined serving platter.

Combine remaining ingredients in a small mixing bowl; mix lightly with a wire whisk. Spoon dressing over salad. Yield: 12 servings.

BLACK BEANS AND RICE CASSEROLE

1 cup dried black beans, uncooked
1 small onion, peeled
1 medium tomato, peeled
1 bay leaf
1 cup cubed, lean, boneless pork steak
¼ cup plus 2 tablespoons olive oil, divided
¾ cup chopped onion
½ cup cubed, cooked ham
½ cup chopped green pepper
1 clove garlic, minced
1 teaspoon dried whole oregano
1½ cups regular rice, uncooked
1½ teaspoons salt
⅛ teaspoon pepper
⅛ teaspoon hot sauce
⅛ teaspoon garlic powder
2 tablespoons lemon juice
1 tablespoon dry vermouth
Fresh parsley sprigs (optional)

Sort beans, and rinse thoroughly. Combine beans and water to cover 2 inches above beans in a large Dutch oven; cover and let stand overnight. Add whole onion, tomato, bay leaf, and additional water, if necessary, to cover 1 inch above beans. Bring to a boil. Reduce heat; cover and simmer 2 hours or until beans are tender. Drain beans, reserving liquid. Add water to liquid to yield 3 cups. Pour liquid over beans, and set aside. Discard onion, tomato, and bay leaf.

Brown pork on all sides in 2 tablespoons hot olive oil in a large skillet. Reduce heat; cover and cook 15 minutes.

Add 2 additional tablespoons olive oil to skillet. Stir in chopped onion, ham, green pepper, garlic, and oregano. Cook, stirring constantly, until vegetables are tender. Stir in rice, salt, pepper, and hot sauce. Cook over low heat 10 minutes, stirring often.

Stir rice mixture into bean mixture in a large Dutch oven. Bring to a boil. Cover and bake at 325° for 30 minutes or until rice is tender.

Heat garlic powder and remaining olive oil in a small skillet. Stir into bean mixture. Add lemon juice and vermouth, toss lightly. Spoon mixture into a 3-quart serving dish. Garnish with parsley sprigs, if desired. Yield: 12 servings.

CUBAN BREAD

6 cups all-purpose flour, divided
2 packages dry yeast
2 cups water
2 tablespoons sugar
2 teaspoons salt
Yellow cornmeal

Combine 2 cups flour and yeast in a large mixing bowl; mix well, and set aside.

Combine water, sugar, and salt in a saucepan; cook over high heat, stirring frequently, until mixture reaches 120° to 130° on candy thermometer. Add to flour mixture; stir until dry ingredients are moistened and dough forms a soft ball. Beat at high speed of an electric mixer 3 minutes or until smooth. Add enough flour to make a stiff dough.

Turn dough out onto a lightly floured surface, and knead 12 minutes or until dough is smooth and elastic.

Place dough in a greased bowl, turning to grease top. Cover and let rise in a warm place (85°), free from drafts, 45 minutes or until dough is doubled in bulk.

Divide dough into 3 portions;

roll each portion into a 13- x 10-inch rectangle. Roll up each rectangle jellyroll fashion, starting at long end. Pinch seams and ends together to seal.

Grease 2 baking sheets, and sprinkle lightly with cornmeal. Place loaves, seam side down, on prepared baking sheets.

Cut 4 to 5 diagonal slashes, ¾-inch-deep, in top of each loaf. Brush with water. Cover and repeat rising procedure 20 minutes or until doubled in bulk. Bake at 400° for 45 minutes (do not preheat oven) or until loaves sound hollow when tapped. Cool bread immediately on wire racks. Yield: 3 loaves.

Note: Baked loaves may be frozen and thawed for later use.

SPANISH FLAN

4 cups sugar, divided
½ cup water
9 eggs
1½ teaspoons vanilla extract
½ teaspoon anisette liqueur
⅛ teaspoon salt
3 cups hot milk (185°)

Combine 1 cup sugar and water in a heavy saucepan. Bring to a boil. Boil, uncovered, 10 minutes or until lightly browned. Pour caramel mixture evenly into 12 buttered 6-ounce custard cups. Set aside.

Beat eggs until thick and lemon colored. Add remaining sugar, vanilla, anisette, and salt, beating well. Gradually add hot milk, beating constantly. Pour milk mixture evenly over caramel mixture in custard cups. Place custard cups in 2 pans of hot water. Bake at 350° for 50 minutes or until a knife inserted in center comes out clean. Chill thoroughly.

Loosen edges with a spatula. Invert flans onto serving plates. Yield: 12 servings.

Clockwise: Cuban Bread, Spanish Boliche with Carrots, Florida Grapefruit-Avocado Salad, Black Beans and Rice Casserole, and Spanish Flan.

cACKNOWLEDGMENTS

Apples Special, Hot Biscuits, Riced Eggs adapted from *Hermitage Cooking, Old and New* by The Ladies Hermitage Association, Hermitage, Tennessee.

Arkansas Tailgate Picnic menu based on recipes adapted from *Prairie Harvest*, by St. Peter's Episcopal Churchwomen, Tollville, Arkansas. By permission of St. Peter's Episcopal Churchwomen, Hazen, Arkansas.

Bar Mitzvah Cake, Fruit Strudel, Bar Mitzvah Brownies, Lemon Bars, Noodle Kugel adapted from *Keneseth Israel Sisterhood Cookbook* by Keneseth Israel Sisterhood, ©1971. By permission of Keneseth Israel Sisterhood, Louisville, Kentucky.

Beet Salad with Pickled Herring, Bread and Butter Pickles, Lefse, Norwegian Meat Roll, Rosettes, Salmon Mold, Scandinavian Meatballs, Sweet Soup adapted from *From Norse Kitchens*. Courtesy of Our Savior's Lutheran Church Women, Clifton, Texas.

Belle Meade Mansion Stuffed Ham, Hayden Salad adapted from *Original Belle Meade Mansion Cookbook*. Courtesy of Belle Meade Mansion, Nashville, Tennessee.

Black Beans and Rice Casserole, Cuban Bread, Spanish Boliche with Carrots adapted from *Jane Nickerson's Florida Cookbook*, ©1973. By permission of University Presses of Florida, Gainesville, Florida.

Cabbage Slaw courtesy of Mrs. Linda Baird Riggs, Nashville, Tennessee.

Carne Guisada on Rice, Refried Black Beans adapted from *The Melting Pot: Ethnic Cuisine in Texas* by The Institute of Texan Cultures, ©1977. By permission of The University of Texas Institute of Texan Cultures, San Antonio, Texas.

Challah courtesy of Bailee Kronowitz, Savannah, Georgia.

Chicken and Dumplings, Individual Liver Paté on Toast Rounds, Roast Tenderloin of Beef with Mushrooms, Tomatoes Stuffed with Spinach Rockefeller adapted from *Southern Sideboards*, compiled by The Junior League of Jackson, ©1978. By permission of The Junior League of Jackson, Mississippi.

Chocolate Delights, Marinated Vegetable Salad adapted from *Georgia Heritage - Treasured Recipes*, © 1979. By permission of The National Society of The Colonial Dames of America in the State of Georgia, Huntsville, Georgia.

Christmas Cookies, Lebkuchen, Lemon Cookies adapted from *Guten Appetit!*, compiled by The Sophienburg Museum, ©1978. By permission of The Sophienburg Museum, New Braunfels, Texas.

Christmas Eggnog courtesy of Mr. and Mrs. J. Balfour Miller, Hope Farm, Natchez, Mississippi.

Corn Light Bread courtesy of Anne Whitaker Smith, Belle Meade Mansion, Nashville, Tennessee.

Cranberry-Cumberland Sauce courtesy of Mrs. Mac Greer, Mobile, Alabama.

Easy Blackberry Cobbler, Gram's Tea Cakes adapted from *The Nashville Cookbook* by Nashville Area Home Economics Association. By permission of Nashville Area Home Economics Association, Nashville, Tennessee.

Florida Grapefruit-Avocado Salad by Mrs. P.J. Scudder, Party Poppy Seed Rolls by Mrs. Glen Evins, Spanish Flan by Columbia Restaurant adapted from *The Gasparilla Cookbook* by The Junior League of Tampa, ©1961. By permission of The Junior League of Tampa.

Fresh Peach Ice Cream, Tennessee Jam Cake courtesy of Peggy M. Smith, Smyrna, Tennessee.

Greek New Year's Dinner based on recipes adapted from *It's Greek to Me* by the Annunciation Greek Orthodox Church, ©1981. By permission of Annunciation Greek Orthodox Church, Memphis, Tennessee.

Grits Soufflé, Tennessee Turkey Hash adapted from *By the Board* by The Ladies Hermitage Association, Hermitage, Tennessee.

Jingle Bread Coffee Cake adapted from *Fredericksburg Home Kitchen Cookbook*, published by The Fredericksburg Home Kitchen Cook Book Central Committee.

June Bridal Luncheon menu based on recipes from *Recipes and Party Plans, A Cookbook for the Hostess* by Sadie LeSeuer.

Layered Caviar Mold, Meatballs in Wine Gravy, Shrimp and Crabmeat Mousse adapted from *Talk About Good!*, compiled by the Junior League of Lafayette, Inc., ©1969. By permission of The Junior League of Lafayette, Louisiana.

Mango Custard courtesy of Javier's Restaurant, Dallas, Texas.

Mexican Happy New Year menu and text courtesy of the Mariano Martinez Family, Dallas, Texas.

Middleton Place Christmas Dinner menu, recipes, and location courtesy of Greg and Nancy Allen, Middleton Place Restaurant, Middleton Place, National Historic Landmark, Charleston, South Carolina.

Mother's Day Brunch menu based on recipes adapted from *Atlanta Cooks for Company* by The Junior Associates of the Atlanta Music Club, ©1968. By permission of The Junior Associates of the Atlanta Music Club, Atlanta.

Mushroom-Onion Custard, Persimmon Pudding adapted from *Christmas in Oklahoma*, compiled and edited by Linda Kennedy Rosser, ©1982. By permission of Bobwhite Publications, Oklahoma City, Oklahoma.

Oklahoma Oyster Supper based on recipes adapted from *Pioneer Cookery Around Oklahoma*, compiled and edited by Linda Kennedy Rosser, ©1978. By permission of Bobwhite Publications, Oklahoma City, Oklahoma.

Pineapple Pie courtesy of Mrs. Woodrow Baird, Mt. Juliet, Tennessee.

Raisin Bread by Mrs. Irene Zittrauer Morgan, courtesy of JoAnne Morgan Conaway, Springfield, Georgia.

Red Cabbage and Apples, Jewish Sabbath Dinner menu based on recipes adapted from *Good Cooks Never Lack Friends* by Sisterhood Agudath Achim Synagogue, ©1978. By permission of Sisterhood of Congregation Agudath Achim, Savannah, Georgia.

Southern Maryland Easter Dinner based on recipes from Mary Clair Matthews, The Hermitage, LaPlata, Maryland.

Spiced Hot Tea courtesy of Mrs. Ralph Lynn, Waco, Texas.

Stuffed Artichokes Sicilian, Tomato Vermicelli Soufflé, Veal Scallopini courtesy of Tony Cannarella Mathews, Savannah, Georgia.

Sunday Dinner at the Purefoy Hotel menu adapted from dishes once served at the Purefoy Hotel, Talladega, Alabama.

Tortilla Soup by Elizabeth Graham Hill, Austin, Texas, first appeared in *Cook 'em Horns* by The Ex-Students' Association of The University of Texas, ©1981. By permission of The Ex-Students' Association, The University of Texas, Austin.

Vanilla Crescents adapted from *Forgotten Recipes*, compiled and updated by Jaine Rodack, ©1981. By permission of Wimmer Bros. Books, Memphis, Tennessee.

Vanilla Ice Cream courtesy of Mrs. R.J. Burch, Jr., Birmingham, Alabama.

Whole Wheat Angel Biscuits adapted from *Favorite Recipes from the Big House* by the N.G. Davis Family, ©1981. By permission of Cookbook Publishers, Inc., Lenexa, Kansas.

INDEX

Almond-Coconut Filling, 117
Ambrosia, 57
Appetizers
    Angels on Horseback, 24
    Caviar Mold, Layered, 91
    Celery, Stuffed, 121
    Cheese Bells, 115
    Cheese Flambé, Fried, 62
    Cheese Straws,
        Old-Fashioned, 125
    Dip, Garlic-Mayonnaise, 95
    Dip, Hot Artichoke, 88
    Dip, Sour Cream Spinach, 115
    Liver Mold, Chopped, 129
    Meatballs in Wine Gravy, 91
    Meatballs, Scandinavian, 18
    Meat Roll, Norwegian, 19
    Oysters, Deviled, 25
    Oysters, Fried, 25
    Pâté on Toast Rounds, Individual
        Liver, 73
    Salmon Mold, 19
    Salmon Mold with Bagels,
        Smoked, 97
    Sandwiches, Chicken, 27
    Sandwiches, Cucumber-Cream
        Cheese, 28
    Sandwiches, Egg Salad
        Finger, 84
    Sandwiches, Noisette, 42
    Sandwiches, Olive-Mustard, 28
    Shrimp with Red Sauce,
        Boiled, 91
    Vegetable Bowl, Fresh, 95
Apples
    Cabbage and Apples, Red, 21
    Noodle Kugel, 97
    Special, Apples, 112
Apricots
    Balls, Apricot, 96
    Sherbet, Apricot, 127
    Tarts, Apricot Cream, 29
Artichokes
    Dip, Hot Artichoke, 88
    Stuffed Artichokes Sicilian, 133
Asparagus
    Casserole, Asparagus, 126
    Lemon Butter, Asparagus
        with, 110

Steamed Asparagus,
    Chilled, 103
Aspics, Individual Tomato, 107
Avocado Salad, Florida
    Grapefruit-, 135

Bacon
    Angels on Horseback, 24
    Biscuits, Bacon, 49
    Canadian Bacon Special, 78
Banana-Fruit Ice Cream, 82
Barbecue
    Chicken, Saucy
        Oven-Barbecued, 88
    Pork Shoulder, Barbecued, 15
Beans
    Baked Beans, 75
    Black Beans and Rice
        Casserole, 136
    Black Beans, Refried, 132
    Butter Beans, 121
    Green
        Country Green Beans, 11
        Italienne, Green Beans, 55
        Salad, Piquant Green Bean, 32
Beef
    Carne Guisada on Rice, 131
    Cholent, 129
    Jerky, Sliced Beef, 44
    Meatballs in Wine Gravy, 91
    Meatballs, Scandinavian, 18
    Meat Roll, Norwegian, 19
    Pot Roast, 125
    Roast Tenderloin of Beef with
        Mushrooms, 73
    Rolls, Cabbage, 129
    Sandwiches, Hero, 69
    Sauerbraten, 22
    Spanish Boliche with
        Carrots, 135
Beet Salad with Pickled
    Herring, 19
Beverages
    Alcoholic
        Andrew Jackson Cooler, 92
        Eggnog, Christmas, 50
        Margaritas, 131
        Peach Daiquiri, 78
        Punch, Champagne, 118

Punch, Fruited
    Champagne, 86
Punch, Planter's, 92
Cranberry Juice Cocktail, 105
Hot Chocolate, 59
Lemonade, 17
Pineapple Orangeade, 68
Punch, Golden Mint, 86
Punch, Wedding, 118
Tea, Spiced Hot, 29
Biscuits
    Bacon Biscuits, 49
    Buttermilk Biscuits, 56
    English Biscuits with Cinnamon
        Butter, 42
    Hot Biscuits, 112
    Supreme, Biscuits, 35
    Whole Wheat Angel Biscuits, 95
    Yeast Biscuits, Fluffy, 12
Blackberries
    Cobbler, Easy Blackberry, 123
    Sauce, Blackberry, 104
Bran Muffins, 127
Bread and Butter Pickles, 20
Breads. See also specific types.
    Chocolate Mandel Bread, 130
    Tortillas, Flour, 132
    Vasilopeta (Greek Sweet
        Bread), 64
    Yeast
        Challah, 130
        Coffee Cake, Jingle Bread, 51
        Cuban Bread, 136
        French Bread, 39
        Greek Bread, 63
        Homemade Yeast Loaves, 45
        Raisin Bread, 22
        Rice Bread, Brown, 31
        Sally Lunn, 122
Brussels Sprouts with Maître
    d'Hôtel Sauce, 39
Buñuelos, 59
Butter, Cinnamon, 42

Cabbage
    Red Cabbage and Apples, 21
    Rolls, Cabbage, 129
    Salad, Hayden, 12
    Salad, Perfection, 76

Cabbage, (continued)
  Slaw, Cabbage, 16
Cakes. *See also* Breads, Cookies.
  Angel Food Cake with Ice Cream
    Balls, 77
  Bar Mitzvah Cake, 101
  Birthday Cake, Sweet
    Sixteen, 70
  Birthday Layer Cake, 77
  Bride's Cake, 117
  Chocolate Cake, Choo-Choo, 67
  Chocolate Delights, 89
  Coconut Pound Cake, 89
  Coffee Cake, Jingle
    Bread, 51
  Devil's Food Cake, 13
  Fruit Cake, Japanese, 57
  Groom's Cake, 118
  Jam Cake, Tennessee, 17
  Lemon Gold Cake, 84
  Lemon Squares, 26
  Little Fancy Cakes, 42
  Pineapple Cake, 123
  Silver Anniversary Cake, 83
  Spice Bars, Frosted, 32
  Vasilopeta (Greek Sweet
    Bread), 64
Candies
  Mint Roses, 84
  Mint Twists, 115
  Pralines, Peanut, 92
Cantaloupe Lilies with Melon
  Balls, 109
Caramel Ice Cream, 81
Carrots
  Ginger Carrots, 55
  Spanish Boliche with
    Carrots, 135
  Spicy Carrots, 129
Casseroles
  Asparagus Casserole, 126
  Beans, Baked, 75
  Black Beans and Rice
    Casserole, 136
  Macaroni au Gratin, 40
  Noodle Kugel, 97
  Rice, Baked Wild, 127
  Riced Eggs, 112
  Rice, Wild, 48
  Squash Casserole, 16, 76
  Tomatoes, Scalloped, 121
Cauliflower à la Vinaigrette, 39
Caviar Mold, Layered, 91
Celery, Stuffed, 121
Challah, 130
Cheese
  Bells, Cheese, 115
  Cooked Cheese, 45
  Dressing, 98
  Fried Cheese Flambé, 62
  Gorgonzola Pears, 134
  Macaroni au Gratin, 40
  Mint Roses, 84
  Sandwiches, Cucumber-Cream
    Cheese, 28
  Sandwiches, Hero, 69
  Sandwiches, Noisette, 42
  Straws, Old-Fashioned
    Cheese, 125

Chicken
  Baked Chicken with Wine and
    Mushrooms, 109
  Creamed Chicken in Patty
    Shells, 104
  Dumplings, Chicken and, 121
  Fried Chicken, Texas, 75
  Liver Mold, Chopped, 129
  Liver Pâté on Toast Rounds,
    Individual, 73
  Oven-Barbecued Chicken,
    Saucy, 88
  Roast Chicken, 126
  Sandwiches, Chicken, 27
  Skillet-Fried Chicken,
    Tennessee, 15
Chocolate
  Bread, Chocolate Mandel, 130
  Brownies, Bar Mitzvah, 99
  Cake, Choo-Choo Chocolate, 67
  Cake, Devil's Food, 13
  Delights, Chocolate, 89
  Frosting, Chocolate, 67
  Frosting, Chocolate-Bourbon, 99
  Hot Chocolate, 59
  Sauce, Chocolate, 82
Cholent, 129
Cobbler, Easy Blackberry, 123
Coconut
  Ambrosia, 57
  Cake, Coconut Pound, 89
  Filling, Almond-Coconut, 117
  Coffee Cake, Jingle Bread, 51
Consommé, Sherried, 73
Cookies
  Arkansas Travelers, 32
  Brownies, Bar Mitzvah, 99
  Chocolate Mandel Bread, 130
  Christmas Cookies, 45
  Gingersnaps, 23
  Highland Cookies, 42
  Icebox Cookies, 82
  Lebkuchen, 46
  Lemon Bars, 98
  Lemon Cookies, 45
  Monogrammed Cookies, 118
  Pfeffernüsse, 46
  Tea Cakes, Gram's, 122
  Vanilla Crescents, 96
Corn-on-the-Cob, 11
Cornbreads
  Buttermilk Cornbread, 122
  Corn Light Bread, 12
  Corn Sticks, 76
  Hush Puppies, 26
Crabmeat Mousse, Shrimp
  and, 103
Cranberries
  Cocktail, Cranberry Juice, 105
  Relish, Cranberry-Orange, 56
  Sauce, Cranberry-
    Cumberland, 38
Cucumbers
  Pickles, Bread and Butter, 20
  Sandwiches, Cucumber-Cream
    Cheese, 28
Custard, Mango, 132
Custard, Mushroom-Onion, 49
Custard Pie, Sweet Potato, 23

Date Pudding, 127
Desserts. *See also* specific types.
  Ambrosia, 57
  Apricot Balls, 96
  Buñuelos, 59
  Diples (Rolled Honey
    Pastry), 64
  Krum Kake, 20
  Meringue Hearts with Pastel
    Sherbets, Pale Green, 110
  Pears, Gorgonzola, 134
  Rosettes, 20
  Sauce, Chocolate, 82
  Sauce, Peanut Butter, 82
  Spanish Flan, 136
  Strawberry Delight, 107
  Strudel, Fruit, 101
Dumplings, Chicken and, 121

Eggnog, Christmas, 50
Eggs
  Brandied Cream Sauce, Eggs
    with, 79
  Deviled Eggs, Frilly, 35
  Dressed Eggs, Turkey Feet, 13
  Eggnog, Christmas, 50
  Riced Eggs, 112
  Salad, Egg, 97
  Sandwiches, Egg Salad
    Finger, 84
  Sandwiches, Olive-Mustard, 28

Fish
  Salmon Mold, 19
  Salmon Mold with Bagels,
    Smoked, 97
  Trout, Fried, 25
Frostings, Fillings, and Toppings
  Almond-Coconut Filling, 117
  Buttercream Frosting, 117
  Butter Frosting, 77
  Butter Frosting, Fluffy, 70
  Chocolate-Bourbon Frosting, 99
  Chocolate Frosting, 67
  Divinity Frosting, 83
  Filling, 57
  Fluffy White Frosting, 13
  Frosting, 17, 32, 42, 57, 101
  Icing, 118
  Icing, Decorator, 67
  Lemon Butter Cream
    Frosting, 84
  Pineapple Frosting, 123
Fruit. *See also* specific types.
  Ambrosia, 57
  Cake, Groom's, 118
  Cake, Japanese Fruit, 57
  Ice Cream, Banana-Fruit, 82
  Punch, Fruited Champagne, 86
  Salad, Fresh Fruit, 76
  Strudel, Fruit, 101

Gingersnaps, 23
Grape Leaves, Stuffed, 61
Grapefruit-Avocado Salad,
  Florida, 135
Grits Soufflé, 112

Ham
  Fried Ham with Cream
    Gravy, 75
  Stuffed Ham, Belle Meade
    Mansion, 11
  Stuffed Ham, Southern
    Maryland, 34
Hash, Tennessee Turkey, 111
Hero Sandwiches, 69
Hush Puppies, 26

Ice Creams and Sherbets
  Apricot Sherbet, 127
  Banana-Fruit Ice Cream, 82
  Caramel Ice Cream, 81
  Peach Ice Cream, Fresh, 17
  Pineapple Sherbet, 40
  Vanilla Ice Cream, 81

Jams and Jellies
  Cake, Tennessee Jam, 17
  Plum Jelly, Fresh, 48

Lefse, 20
Lemon
  Bars, Lemon, 98
  Butter, Asparagus with
    Lemon, 110
  Cake, Lemon Gold, 84
  Cookies, Lemon, 45
  Frosting, Lemon Butter
    Cream, 84
  Lemonade, 17
  Squares, Lemon, 26
Liver Mold, Chopped, 129
Liver Pâté on Toast Rounds,
  Individual, 73

Macaroni au Gratin, 40
Mango Custard, 132
Meatballs
  Scandinavian Meatballs, 18
  Wine Gravy, Meatballs in, 91
Meat Roll, Norwegian, 19
Melon Balls, Cantaloupe Lilies
  with, 109
Meringue Hearts with Pastel
  Sherbets, Pale Green, 110
Mint Punch, Golden, 86
Mint Roses, 84
Mint Twists, 115
Mousse, Shrimp and
  Crabmeat, 103
Muffins
  Bran Muffins, 127
  Pecan Muffins, Georgia, 79
  Tea Muffins, 112
Mushrooms
  Baked Chicken with Wine and
    Mushrooms, 109
  Custard, Mushroom-Onion, 49
  Roast Tenderloin of Beef with
    Mushrooms, 73

Noodle Kugel, 97

Okra, Fried, 16
Olive-Mustard Sandwiches, 28
Onion Custard, Mushroom-, 49

Oranges
  Ambrosia, 57
  Pineapple Orangeade, 68
  Relish, Cranberry-Orange, 56
Oysters
  Angels on Horseback, 24
  Deviled Oysters, 25
  Fried Oysters, 25
  Stew, Oyster, 53
  Stuffing, Roast Turkey with
    Oyster, 38

Peaches
  Daiquiri, Peach, 78
  Ice Cream, Fresh Peach, 17
Peanut Butter Sauce, 82
Peanut Pralines, 92
Pears
  Gorgonzola Pears, 134
  Salad, Pear, 127
Peas
  Black-Eyed Pea Salad, 62
  Confetti Rice, 109
  Green Peas, 48
  Green Peas, Creamed, 126
Pecans
  Muffins, Georgia Pecan, 79
  Pie, Georgia Pecan, 23
  Salted Pecans, 86
  Stuffing, Roast Turkey with
    Rice-Pecan, 54
  Tarts, Pecan, 28
Peppers, Italian Roasted, 134
Persimmon Pudding, 49
Pfeffernüsse, 46
Pickled Herring, Beet Salad
  with, 19
Pickles, Bread and Butter, 20
Pies and Pastries
  Blackberry Cobbler, Easy, 123
  Buñuelos, 59
  Chicken in Patty Shells,
    Creamed, 104
  Diples (Rolled Honey Pastry), 64
  Fruit Strudel, 101
  Osgood Pie, 13
  Pastry, 28
  Pecan Pie, Georgia, 23
  Pineapple Pie, 17
  Spinach Pie, 62
  Sweet Potato Custard Pie, 23
  Tarts, Apricot Cream, 29
  Tarts, Pecan, 28
Pineapple
  Cake, Pineapple, 123
  Frosting, Pineapple, 123
  Orangeade, Pineapple, 68
  Pie, Pineapple, 17
  Sherbet, Pineapple, 40
Plum Jelly, Fresh, 48
Plum Pudding, 40
Pork
  Barbecued Pork Shoulder, 15
  Meatballs, Scandinavian, 18
  Meat Roll, Norwegian, 19
  Roast Pork with Potatoes,
    Grecian-Style, 62
  Sandwiches, Razorback
    Roast, 30

Potatoes
  Lefse, 20
  Red Potatoes, Creamed, 34
  Roast Pork with Potatoes,
    Grecian-Style, 62
  Salad, Hot German
    Potato, 22
  Salad, Sour Cream-Mustard
    Potato, 89
Potatoes, Sweet
  Pie, Sweet Potato Custard, 23
Pralines, Peanut, 92
Prunes, Stuffed, 127
Puddings
  Cardinal Pudding, 36
  Date Pudding, 127
  Mango Custard, 132
  Persimmon Pudding, 49
  Plum Pudding, 40
  Rum Pudding with Blackberry
    Sauce, 104
  Spanish Flan, 136

Quail, Holiday Baked, 48

Raisins
  Bread, Raisin, 22
  Soup, Sweet, 18
Relishes
  Cranberry-Orange Relish, 56
  Hayden Salad, 12
Rice
  Baked Wild Rice, 127
  Bread, Brown Rice, 31
  Carne Guisada on Rice, 131
  Casserole, Black Beans and
    Rice, 136
  Confetti Rice, 109
  Stuffing, Roast Turkey with
    Rice-Pecan, 54
  Wild Rice, 48
Rolls and Buns. See also Breads.
  Crescent Rolls, 107
  Poppy Seed Rolls, Party, 115
Rum Pudding with Blackberry
  Sauce, 104

Salads and Salad Dressings
  Beet Salad with Pickled
    Herring, 19
  Black-Eyed Pea Salad, 62
  Cantaloupe Lilies with Melon
    Balls, 109
  Confetti Rice, 109
  Dressing, 98
  Egg Salad, 97
  Egg Salad Finger
    Sandwiches, 84
  Fruit Salad, Fresh, 76
  Grapefruit-Avocado Salad,
    Florida, 135
  Green Bean Salad, Piquant, 32
  Hayden Salad, 12
  Pear Salad, 127
  Perfection Salad, 76
  Potato Salad, Hot German, 22
  Potato Salad, Sour
    Cream-Mustard, 89
  Prunes, Stuffed, 127

Salads (continued)
  Relish, Cranberry-Orange, 56
  Slaw, Cabbage, 16
  Tomato Aspics, Individual, 107
  Vegetable Salad, Marinated, 89
  Vegetable Salad, Seven-Layer
    Congealed, 98
Sally Lunn, 122
Salmon
  Mold, Salmon, 19
  Mold with Bagels, Smoked
    Salmon, 97
Sandwiches
  Chicken Sandwiches, 27
  Cucumber-Cream Cheese
    Sandwiches, 28
  Egg Salad Finger
    Sandwiches, 84
  Hero Sandwiches, 69
  Noisette Sandwiches, 42
  Olive-Mustard Sandwiches, 28
  Roast Sandwiches,
    Razorback, 30
Sauces and Gravies
  Blackberry Sauce, 104
  Brandied Cream Sauce, 79
  Chocolate Sauce, 82
  Cranberry-Cumberland
    Sauce, 38
  Cream Gravy, Fried Ham
    with, 75
  Hard Sauce, 49
  Hard Sauce, Sherried, 40
  Maître d'Hôtel Sauce, Brussels
    Sprouts with, 39
  Peanut Butter Sauce, 82
  Red Sauce, Boiled Shrimp
    with, 91

Seafood Sauce, 26
  Tartar Sauce, 25
  Wine Gravy, Meatballs in, 91
Sauerbraten, 22
Scallopini, Veal, 133
Shrimp
  Boiled Shrimp with Red
    Sauce, 91
  Cardinal Sauce, Shrimp in, 105
  Mousse, Shrimp and
    Crabmeat, 103
Slaw, Cabbage, 16
Soufflés
  Grits Soufflé, 112
  Tomato Vermicelli Soufflé, 134
Soups and Stews
  Carne Guisada on Rice, 131
  Consommé, Sherried, 73
  Oyster Stew, 53
  Sweet Soup, 18
  Tomato Soup, 94
  Tortilla Soup, 131
Spinach
  Dip, Sour Cream Spinach, 115
  Pie, Spinach, 62
  Tomatoes Stuffed with Spinach
    Rockefeller, 73
Squash Casserole, 16, 76
Strawberry Delight, 107
Stuffings and Dressings
  Oyster Stuffing, Roast Turkey
    with, 38
  Rice-Pecan Stuffing, Roast
    Turkey with, 54
Sweet Potato Custard Pie, 23
Syrup, Simple, 92

Tarts
  Apricot Cream Tarts, 29
  Pecan Tarts, 28
Tomatoes
  Aspics, Individual Tomato, 107
  Baked Tomato Halves, 35
  Scalloped Tomatoes, 121
  Soufflé, Tomato Vermicelli, 134
  Soup, Tomato, 94
  Spinach Rockefeller, Tomatoes
    Stuffed with, 73
Tortillas
  Flour Tortillas, 132
  Soup, Tortilla, 131
Trout, Fried, 25
Turkey
  Hash, Tennessee Turkey, 111
  Oyster Stew, 54
  Roast Turkey with Oyster
    Stuffing, 38
  Roast Turkey with Rice-Pecan
    Stuffing, 54

Vanilla Crescents, 96
Vanilla Ice Cream, 81
Veal
  Loaf, Congealed Veal, 95
  Scallopini, Veal, 133
Vegetables. See also specific types.
  Bowl, Fresh Vegetable, 95
  Salad, Marinated Vegetable, 89
  Salad, Seven-Layer Congealed
    Vegetable, 98

Whole Wheat Angel Biscuits, 95